Myself, Me and I

JO ALLOTT

Debbie.
Hope you enjoy.
Hugs Jo x

MYSELF, ME AND I

JO ALLOTT

Note from the author

This book is based on true events but some names of the characters and locations have been changed.

This book is based entirely on my memories. No memory is infallible, and I'm sure some people will remember things differently, but this is my life through my eyes, and this what I recall. So sit back, take a load off, and I hope you enjoy the bumpy ride.

ISBN-13: 978-1484822586

ISBN-10: 1484822587

MYSELF, ME AND I

Dedication

This book is dedicated to each person out there who is suffering with bulimia. In particular, I offer you Chapter Twelve, Sugar Coating, for those words, although they fit my own situation and my personal story, they do not belong to me; they are the unspoken words of each and every one of you. I hope one day that you will read this book, learn from my mistakes and find the strength to get the help you need. You are unique, you are loved, and you are wonderful; you deserve to be happy.

MYSELF, ME AND I

Acknowledgements

I have so many people in my life that I am thankful for.

Mum, I love and respect you, and owe you so much. You have always been there for me even when I have been a complete nightmare and have pushed you away. Thank you.

Kelli, what more could I ask for in a sister? You took my shitty behaviour and came back for more; you have been a good friend as well as a sister, and I love you all the more for that.

My wonderful friends - Jennie, Becky, Joy, Davie, Steve, Sylvie, Liam, Vicky, Simon, Debbie, Carole, Sarah and Ant - I thank each and every one of you for being a part of my life. You have supported me through the good, the bad and the ugly and I truly appreciate your faith in me and your continued love and support.

Ian, naturally I owe you special thanks for your hug. Until recently you had no idea just how much it had meant to me, but I know you now understand. I will never be able to thank you enough for that simple life-changing (life-saving) act of kindness.

The beautiful and talented Kerry Newman, thank you for turning my words into something I could share. Without you and your understanding of my food battles, my thoughts and memories on paper would never have become this book.

Finally, and strangely, I thank Annie - my eating disorder. You had the ability to be my destroyer but you ended up being my saviour. Without the lessons you taught me, I wouldn't be where I am or be who I am today.

JO ALLOTT

Chapters

Introduction

July 3rd, 2012

Okay I am only on the introduction and I have writer's block already! The notion that I can write a book, I mean *really* write a book. Me?! It perplexes me beyond all belief. Because I'm just a prison officer from Buckinghamshire, who left school many years ago with just two GCSE passes; I am not a journalist, an author, or even a writer. I have absolutely no writing experience of any kind. So the concept that I can actually pull this off? Well at the moment I think I might actually have more chance of climbing Mount Everest wearing nothing but a bikini and flip flops, then rolling down the other side screaming "Weeeee!"

Why were we on that train together again on Thursday? It hit me like a bolt of lightning while I was out running the following morning . . .

Now I know this may sound totally insane and you will probably laugh, but this man appears in my life at random intervals; he is not an active part of my life in any way, shape or form. But on that run I suddenly felt that fate had brought us together again for a reason. I'm a great believer in that kind of thing philosophically, to the point that I'm beginning to wonder if not only is he a friend; but might he be my Guardian Angel, appearing in my life when I need him most – Oooh, the DEEPNESS of the Allott brain!

June 28th, 2012

I was on the train on my way back from a business meeting in East Croydon. I've taken that journey maybe a dozen times in the past year and only bumped in to him twice. Both times he has helped me, without realising it, with 'vocal hugs' in the form of advice. This time was weird, I mean REALLY weird. Before he got on the train I was working away and not even thinking about anything but work. I was busy working out the potential profit margins for a wedding event I had just secured.

I couldn't believe what my calculator was telling me and was sure I must have pressed a wrong key, so I did the whole calculation again. The same figure appeared. I then leant my head back, onto the headrest of my train seat; as there were so many things going through my mind . . .

- I could not believe what I was seeing. The potential profit was FANTASTIC!

- How ON EARTH was little old me going to cook for an event this big?

- My business is taking off faster than I planned.

- Where the hell am I going to prepare and cook all this food? My kitchen's certainly not big enough!

- What happens to my full time job, if my business continues to expand so quickly? It scares me to think of quitting because of the guaranteed salary, which I need.

- Jo, what on earth are you going to do?

All these thoughts were going through my head as the train was slowing to a station. I hadn't been paying attention to the announcements before but as soon as I heard, "This train is now approaching Heathfield Common," I knew he would get on the train and help me again. I even looked straight at the door he used, although there were four, or maybe six, carriages. SPOOKY huh? When he saw me looking his way, he actually asked me if I was expecting him. I didn't say yes, because it's only now I know, as I am writing this down that I was. I realise how nuts it actually sounds, but in those last six seconds I knew he would get on that train, walk through that door and help me again!

This isn't the first time things like this have happened in my life, are they crazy coincidences? Or is there more to it than that? What I do know is as child I could answer the phone and know who was on the end of the line (before caller ID was introduced!). I've dreamt things that have later happened. I've been told three times I'm psychic, twice by a well known medium (who wanted me to attend her development circle) and once last year by someone I met on a prison service training course! I was strangely drawn to Barry, who I later found out was a healer, and I let him 'test' me three times, after which he asked me why I was blocking my natural abilities!

If I am blocking something, there's a very good reason why! Could you imagine walking down A Wing and you see something? As I'm writing this down, I'm actually wondering what the faces of the people that I know look like right now. Hi I'm Jo, and I see dead people! Oh sod it, this book is supposed to be the full story, so here goes: I do think I've already seen a ghost in my life and no, they don't look like the stereotypical image we have of them (but more about that later).

As I was leaving the course and saying goodbye to Barry, he handed me two CDs which he said would open my third eye (?!). I was to listen to them on my own and in the dark. Barry also said that I would contact him once I had listened to them. So I bet you're wondering if I have or haven't listened to them - errrrrrmmmmmm let me see NO, why? Because the notion that this maybe, just maybe is true and I do have some kind of sixth sense scares me shitless!

OK, back to the train journey...

The first time I bumped in to him on the train, I had been given a huge project at work and was on my way back from another prison in London, that I had visited to compare their systems with some proposals I was suggesting for my own establishment. The project I had been given was simply HUMUNGOUS and way over my rank or pay scale! However since I became I, I thrive on the challenges that life throws my way.

MYSELF, ME AND I

During this first journey together, we spoke about my project and I cheekily asked him if I could send him the proof to read so I didn't make myself look stupid when I presented it to my own senior management team. He agreed and reassured me that it would be fine as he knew the quality of my work. He then asked me how I was, because the last time he had seen me I hadn't been in a good place.

All I told him was that I was fine! This in part was true; I was getting there. I'd completed my therapy just a few months earlier and had banished my demons. But I wasn't ready to tell him or anyone my story just yet . . .

This time, as we sat together, we spoke at length about my new business venture and he gave me some really valuable ideas and suggestions that I had not even thought of, but I will be using. He then asked me about the new tattoo which I have on my thumb. What did it say and what did it mean? Because he asked me this question, I felt compelled to tell him the profound effect that his hug had had on me and I began to share some of my life's story and the run up to it.

Having opened up and seen the impact my story had made on him during that train ride, while I was out running the next day I really gave some thought to the significant role he'd unwittingly played in my life and the following week I sent him an email. I asked him if he would come on journey with me, metaphorically speaking. I asked him because, as well as him playing a key role to the person I am now and the fact that I'm even writing a book, I knew he had a background in Psychology and I knew he would be honest with me in my jottings. I guess in essence I was asking if he could spare me another hug, or in fact eighteen: one for each chapter. I had hoped to send him each chapter of this book by email as it was written. Hey, I'm greedy; what can I say?! I have had THE HUG as well as the two later vocal hugs. Do you know I truly believe hugs may be the best medicine in the whole wide world . . .

Unfortunately he was unable at the time to support me with this, due to his own personal circumstances, which was totally fine. I decided the book had to be written anyway, no matter how long it took. I knew it was something that I had to do. I also decided that I would give him the first copy once published.

In this story, I will be brutally honest about everything that has happened in my life. It's very dark at points, but I do want you to see the humour too. The reason I want to write my story down is because if my story helps just one person experiencing a hard life to make a positive change, or it inspires someone to give somebody else a hug (remember, it doesn't cost you anything and it could be life-changing!), then Cursum Percifico: my journey will really be complete.

So, what issues have I overcome on my journey from becoming Myself to I? Let me see, there has been:

1. An Eating Disorder

2. Body Dysmorphic Disorder (BDD)

3. Unhelpful Perfectionism

4. Bullying

5. Depression and Insomnia

6. Alcohol misuse

7. Low self esteem

8. Not knowing who I was as a person

9. Accepting a parent that doesn't love me

If someone asked me three years ago where I saw myself in 2012, my honest answer would have been maggot food!

Yet look at me now - soaring, soaring like an eagle!

So, love me or hate me, both are in my favour! If you love me in your life, I will always be in your heart! If you hate me, I will always be on your mind . . .

Fucked up huh?

The Beginning of Temper Tantrums

July 3rd 2012

I've spoken to my mum this evening. I don't really remember very much about my early years but I thought I should start at the beginning, so I've asked her to fill in some of the gaps. As it turns out, it appears that I've been a pain in her arse almost since the moment I was conceived! Well, why break the habit of a lifetime right . . .

What I did find out was Joanne was a very much wanted daughter, and after a long and slow week of labour, forceps finally dragged me into this world, kicking and screaming in all my naked glory, at 17.20 on Thursday the 17th of August 1978. My parents were Raymond, an electrician working in a coal mine, and Susan, a factory worker. I was born at Kings Mill Hospital near Mansfield and we lived in Huthwaite, which is a small mining village just outside Sutton-in-Ashfield in Nottinghamshire. Huthwaite is made up predominantly of red brick terraced houses and council estates. I remember that it was the type of place, when I was a young child, where everyone knew everyone, and everyone knew everyone else's business; your neighbours' and parents' friends where all known as aunty or uncle and no one ever felt the need to lock their doors. You would think that such a friendly and secure environment would have created a friendly and secure child. Well, I guess I was friendly . . .

MYSELF, ME AND I

My parents could not decide what to call me. My mum wanted Hannah (this fact is worth remembering), after my great grandma, but my dad didn't agree. It was finally decided that I would be called Joanne-Lynn Allott after both my parents' mothers and my dad's sister who died as a child. I am told that I was a contented baby who was Daddy's little princess! As I grew in to a toddler, I caused no problems for my parents. Dad would go off to work and as soon as he came home, no matter what I was doing, I would drop everything and run screaming into his arms for hugs and kisses. When my mum became pregnant with my sister Kelli, I would kiss her expanding belly in excitement and say it was *my* baby! When Kelli was born, I always wanted to feed and help Mum bathe her, I was the model big sister. Everything was great, and life was good. It was only after my dad left home in late 1982 that I became problematic . . .

During our phone call, Mum said she would have to think about some of the things that went on during my later years and mentioned that she would have to go through some old documentation in order to provide the accurate information that I was asking for, such as dates. I asked her what she was talking about and Mum explained that she had kept safe all the key information about me (and Kelli). She had planned to give this to us one day but as yet she hadn't got around to it. I told her I needed to do this myself, and asked her if she would post this information to me.

July 6th, 2012, 6.03pm

I arrived home from work as normal to find my mum's package waiting for me. Erica, my lodger, had left it on the table. I wasn't sure if I was excited or nervous to discover even more about my younger self. I opened the parcel to find what I would describe as a memory box which contained all the key things that Mum wanted me to know about myself - a newspaper clipping from the day I was born, my first tooth, my old school records - you get the drift. It was only then that I found the record: The Commodores, *Three Times A Lady*! I picked this up and looked at it, not understanding why it was actually in the box. I called Mum and asked her why it was there: "Well it was the number one song in the charts the day you were born." she replied. Seriously, are you kidding? I had to do a Google search to confirm it. She was right. What are the chances that I would start writing this book, when the very song on the day I was born is Three Times A Lady?! Another 'coincidence' in my life maybe?

Just looking through this box brought back a flood of forgotten memories that I had no idea I had suppressed so deeply and so well. I did begin question whether I really wanted to take this trip down memory lane and open up this can of old worms . . .

July 6th, 2012, 9.30pm

After some serious soul searching for the past couple of hours, I have decided I really do want to do this.

However, I'm no longer sure that it is a purely selfless act; I wonder if it will provide total closure for me also.

Enough talking about how and why I came to write my story, now . . .

The story begins

August 17th, 1978

Joanne is born

1982

Dad leaves

March, 1984

My earliest childhood memory is around the age of five or six years old and I was in hospital. I had suffered for a while with the most excruciating stomach pains and had trouble going to the toilet. After numerous tests and visits to the doctors, it was discovered that I had a twisted bowel which would require immediate surgery to rectify it. I remember that both Mum and Dad were there, comforting me at the hospital as I screamed and cried. I remember being so scared as they were trying to put me to sleep. I kept pushing the mask away as they put it over my mouth, and wriggling to stop them. I remember my mum having tears in her eyes and my dad held my hands while telling me not to worry, that he would not let anyone hurt me. This was the first time that Mum and Dad had been together with me since they separated and even in my terrified childish mind I knew my mummy and daddy were here and loved me. When I woke up it was just my mum there and so, of course, all I wanted was my dad. (Thinking about this now brings tears to my eyes, as she was the one who has always there for me, not him.) It was not long after this I first started to act up. The first thing that I would do was to hold myself when I needed the toilet so that it would cause pain and I would pretend that I needed to be at the hospital again. My childish belief was that if I went back to hospital, Daddy would be there again with Mummy. When this didn't work I started to create other problems.

I would take things from school pretending they were mine, although I would only keep them for a short while, before returning them the next day. My mum never had much in the way of materialistic possessions and we survived a lot of the time on hand-me-downs from friends and family. I guess I was jealous of those who had what I wanted. I once took a PE bag from another pupil's peg and put it in my bag; of course my mum found this and made me take it back and apologise. Then there were my lies: telling other children I had things that I didn't, just to try and fit in with them. When none of these things brought my mum and dad back together, I then turned my anger to my sister Kelli back at home. Her insecurities were my prey, and I would hunt them down, drag them out and throw them whole heartedly in to her face. It was a cruel game, yes, but the game of a child screaming to be noticed.

MYSELF, ME AND I

We used to play games up in our bedroom and I would hit her if she didn't do what I told her; when she would cry and threaten to tell Mum what I had done I would threaten to hit her even harder. One of my favourite control mechanisms was to tell her what she feared the most: that she would lose me like we had lost our Dad. I suppose in some ways I wanted her to suffer the pain and fear of loss that I felt. I would sit against the wall, rocking backwards and forwards saying "They're coming to take me away." As we got older I began to up the tempo, but she also began to fight back. We laugh at this now and still say the score is 2-1 to me, but she also threatens (hopefully not seriously!) that revenge is a dish best served cold! These are our top three sibling fights (as discussed recently, over a glass or two of wine).

1. Joanne duct-taping Kelli to a dining room chair, while holding her eyes open so she had to watch children being fed through a sausage machine (Pink Floyd's video We Don't Need No Education, from the album The Wall).

2. Joanne singing the Freddy Kruger song to Kelli, who is so scared, she is eventually sick through crying. Mum had to intervene and put Kelli in her bed. Mum then ended up sleeping on the landing floor between the two of us, while I sang all night:

   One, two, Freddy's coming for you
   Three, four, better lock your door.

Five, six, grab a crucifix.
Seven, eight, better stay up late.
*Nine, ten, **never** sleep again*
.

3. Kelli annoying Joanne, while she is doing homework so Joanne then throws some scissors towards Kelli which accidentally hit her, breaking the skin and sticking in to her leg (I really never meant for that to happen, I just wanted to scare her). Kelli then ran out of the house and across the street to tell Mum (who is visiting a friend) what I've done. A few years ago, I found out that en route, as Kelli was running, the scissors fell out; Kelli picked them up and she stuck them back, deeper into her leg, before blaming Joanne. Maybe this means she's the overall winner after all! So no need for revenge, hey sis?!

(Jesus Kelli, I *am* sorry for all the crap I put you through. I am surprised you're still talking to me and will now humbly accept your nick name for me: Psycho Sis).

By this time I had moved up to another school and Kelli used to idolise me; I was her big sister and she wanted to copy everything that I did. I did manipulate her innocence. I always knew from an early age that I was smart and in fact I have often relied on what I think to be a potent combination of book-smarts and a quick tongue to get me out of many a situation. I was the type of kid if you asked me when my birth date was I would reply the seventeenth of August. If you then asked me what year, I would cite every year in turn with a sarcastic smirk. While other kids my age would listen to music by the likes of Kylie and Jason, I was listening to ABBA, REM, the Electric Light Orchestra, Fleetwood Mac, U2 and Pink Floyd.

Perhaps surprisingly, I had lots of friends, mainly because they didn't know that most of what I was telling them was a figment of my over active imagination (for example, my imaginary pet rabbit). We used to all hang out in a small group and spend our out-of-school time in the park next to my house. While my girlfriends would want to play games with dolls, and practice dance routines, I would soon get bored of these and go to find some boys to play with. I was a real tomboy who had very little fear and I much preferred hanging around with the boys, playing British Bull Dog and making dens; I would always be the first to the top of the trees and always pushed myself to get to the highest point. I loved nothing more than helping the boys terrorise the young neighbourhood children, by throwing water bombs and eggs at them.

I remember finding some fluorescent pink size three heels at around the age of ten, while I was out playing one day. I hid these inside my school bag, which I then sneaked into school with me the following day. I was showing them off to some of the other girls at school in the changing rooms over our lunch break and one of them double dared me to climb over the coat racks in them (you know the old fashioned wooden ones with a metal coat hook?). As I went to do this I slipped, yes, the hook went right where you are expecting and hurt like hell! (I'm sat cross-legged just remembering this). I really had hurt myself, but instead of admitting that, I told everyone that I was a woman now because I had started my period! This was when I got the nickname Cherryade Knickers, and the taunting first began. Of course, with hindsight, I can see that I had no one to blame but myself, but that didn't make it any easier to cope with at the time.

I was so mean to my mum sometimes as well as Kelli. I knew what to say to hurt her and so when she tried to challenge or discipline me in any way, I would throw a fit and scream that I did not love her and I wanted to go and live with my dad, before running away to one of my secret dens (until I got cold or hungry enough to go home). I must have used this threat hundreds of times, until Mum finally called my bluff; after one such incident I returned home to find that she had packed my bags while I had been gone. When I asked her what they were, she told me that she had called my dad and if I really wanted to go and live with him then I could – I never ever used this threat again. Although I idolised my dad, and really missed him, I think this made me realise how much I depended on my mum.

Not long after this period of rebellion, I decided to join the Army Cadets. I always loved doing challenging things that other girls didn't or wouldn't do, so while my girlfriends talked about being teachers, nurses and hairdressers, I decided that I wanted to be a soldier when I left school. (Looking back, I wonder whether I was also seeking out the company of boys and men in an attempt to feel closer to my father and to be able to talk to him about things he would be interested in, rather than the girly things my mum and Kelli liked). I loved Army Cadets because I would usually end up muddy and wet while out on some training exercise; it beat sitting in front of the TV, that's for sure. I loved the outdoor lifestyle and the lack of fear in me really got a buzz from the things we did. I would think nothing of rock climbing or abseiling down a rock face, even at the tender age of eleven I would be at the front of the queue asking to be the first to do it. We would also go off on all kinds of expeditions (camping for a few nights in a national park for example) were we would be split into teams and have to hunt for each other, as if were real soldiers. I learnt how to survive in the wilderness, how to cook (something that I would pick up again later), how to light a fire, and how to be a first-aider during my time with Army Cadets. It was through this pastime that I also first discovered my passion for music; I began playing the trumpet and, from that moment on, I wanted to be a soldier in a military band.

I didn't like my long hair, because I believed it gave me the wrong image; if I seriously wanted to be a solider it needed to be short. The next time I was due at the hairdressers, I asked Mum if I could have it shorter and she happily let me go off to my appointment, expecting me to lose the shoulder-length locks and come back with a bob. We used to go to the salon on our own because it was literally across the street. Joanne didn't go for a bob though. I asked for a GI Jane and had a grade one all over. Now I believed I looked like a real solider (Demi Moore definitely rocked this look much, *much* better than I did!). Needless to say, my mum went ballistic when I walked through the door, but I said I didn't care, I liked it. Unfortunately, I liked it for all of about twenty four hours; when I got up the following day for school and it sank in what I had actually done, I wasn't so confident! Looking in the mirror, all I could see was that I really looked like a boy. It was only then that I burst in to tears, because I was stuck with my bad decision until my hair began to grow a reasonable length again, which took months.

Mum knew at this time that I was spiralling out of control and apparently she and her partner Mick, arranged a meeting with my dad and step mum Jan to discuss me, just after the above hair incident. She told Dad what I was getting up to and how this was much worse after my weekly visits to see him. She asked him to help her deal with me. I'm glad I only found this out recently, but it still really hurts; apparently his response was "Get her some professional help; she is not right in the head." Ouch! I am an adult now, and I can see that maybe, I was just a hurting child who felt that no-one understood me, and I was trying to get my parents' attention. It's a shame nobody really worked that out at the time.

So family therapy was arranged, but you already know I was very smart; I was also a very good actor! I did what everyone wanted and expected. I acted dumb, but I knew exactly what to say and do to get out of that room. After about five sessions I was free to continue on with my rampage.

Myself

OK so I had left family therapy in the summer of 1990, the same year that I was moving up to secondary school. As I walked out of the door of the therapist's office for the last time, I realised that I had out-grown my family! I didn't believe that they understood me or that I belonged with them. How does a child reach a conclusion like that at this age? I don't know. I can see now that that is quite a shocking idea for an eleven year old to have (although of course all teenagers experience this to some degree or other as they develop their sense of independence), but at the time it just seemed obvious to me.

I don't want to hurt anyone by revealing these thoughts, but I did promise to share my journey in full. I will never forget my roots or where I've come from, and I do love my family very much, even if I don't say it as often as I should. In fact, Mum has to be one of the most inspirational women that I know. She was a single parent who refused to claim state handouts while bringing up two daughters and working full time to support her family. She was the one who instilled in Kelli and me our ethos of work; appreciating what you have in life and working hard to achieve these rewards. This was apparent all throughout my troubled years (although for many years it was largely materialistic rewards that I was interested in), it just took me until I was in my thirties to really see and appreciate it. After I had left family therapy, I tried to be good, I really did, and for the most part that's how I came across to the outside world. I would wear a perfect big white smile on my face, and I would always say please and thank you when I was supposed to. It was as if one child had walked in to the therapists' office and another, better, version of me left it.

A success all round then? Unfortunately not . . .

Now I knew what was expected of me and how I needed to behave in public and I knew I wasn't 'right'. Because I had turned the anger towards myself and to feel better about myself, I turned to food for comfort. Food didn't ask anything of me. It was safe and reliable. Whenever I felt bad, I would eat and inevitably I began to grow bigger and bigger. When I couldn't find food at home to eat in secret, I would take things from other pupils' lunch boxes at school. I would even steal bars of chocolate from the local shops to fix my food cravings. (Maybe it was destined in the stars that I ended up in a prison; it's certainly amazing to me that I ended up on the right side of the bars!)

September 8th, 1990

This is the day my life changed forever on one of my regular Saturday afternoon visits to see my dad. I had always treasured this time; for me it was the highlight of the week because it meant for just a few hours I was with someone that I believed really loved me. This is one visit that will always remain in my head, but it isn't warm and loving feelings that come to mind! Sure, I had gained a lot of weight, but when the dad you idolise sits you down and tells you this at such a young and impressionable age, it has a huge impact. To add insult to injury, my dad then said he wanted to see how heavy I really was. Ummmmm, not good! But I did as I was told, and climbed on to those white scales, watching the dial spin slowly around before reaching its final destination. It seemed like one of those surreal moments in life that takes forever (a bit like a game of roulette when you are waiting for the ball to land at its winning slot, not knowing if it will be black or red) and then, finally, the result - 11 stone 3 pounds. I was subsequently told "You will never become anything if you are fat, and no one will like you. I will give you a pound in money for every pound in weight that you lose." I think it would probably have hurt me less if he had punched through my rib cage, torn out my heart, thrown it on the floor and stamped on it while telling me "You won't be needing that anymore."

That night I cried so hard in to my pillow for what must have been an eternity. This was the first of what became many, many nights that I have cried myself to sleep over the years. This was the first time Myself ever spoke to Me! I don't mean in the schizophrenic sense, but as I lay in bed that night Annie was born and she promised to help me get thinner, which would mean I was prettier, which would mean my dad would love me again.

The following morning I woke up early to a beautiful and sunny Sunday. I had breakfast at home as normal and then went out for a last play with some of my friends before we all started our new schools the following day. Some of us would be going to the local comprehensive school and others to the local community school. We knew our friendship group would be splitting in two directions, so we had all arranged to have a party and picnic in the park, with each of us bringing some food or drink.

This was the day that I first purged. It had been easy for me to over eat that lunchtime, because I was much bigger than the other kids no one dared to say anything to me. A short while later I pretended that I needed the toilet and headed home. Of course I didn't really have to go home; along the route, I found some trees and behind them is where I first stuck my fingers down my throat. (I had no idea what bulimia was at this point, to this day, I don't know why I or what even made me think to do this.) At first all that happened was I gagged and coughed, with tears stinging my eyes. I kept doing this over and over again until finally, VICTORY, the food left my body.

The following day was my first day of senior school. I remember being so scared because most of my friends had gone to the other community school and I hardly knew anyone that was here. As I arrived at the school I was met with this huge daunting grey building that must have been five times the size of my primary school. We were all ushered in to the assembly hall like cattle at a cattle market - it was so intimidating. I was allocated House Unit Three which was known also as Chesterfield House. There was only one other girl I knew in my whole house group and I didn't know her very well, but we agreed to sit together.

MYSELF, ME AND I

During the first few months Annie would come to me only occasionally, when I felt truly guilty or greedy. She was my little secret and no one could take her away from me. As long as I didn't share Annie, she would help me be thin and pretty. But over the next few months she became stronger and stronger and visited more frequently. I would spend all my dinner money on chocolate, crisps, pasties and pizza. Anything that I wanted to eat I could, because I knew it wouldn't stay inside my body for very long afterwards. At first, I kept this behaviour for school, because it was easy to hide there, but soon, once a day was no longer satisfying Annie enough. I had started to spend all my pocket money on food for my fixes. I would hide this food all around my bedroom, often in my nightdress case. This was designed to look like an Angel and, if you unzipped the back, you could turn it inside out to become a Devil - ironically I guess it symbolised the two sides of me.

Unfortunately, I had to leave the Army Cadets during the first year of senior school. I had begun to notice that the boots I wore really hurt my right foot even when I was just walking. It seemed I was severely flat footed and now had a problem with my right foot that required surgery. My right navicular bone needed to be removed by a specialist surgeon because it stuck out and caused me pain. I was also asthmatic and I was told by the sergeants in the Cadets that because of these issues I would never get in to the Army as I had planned and dreamed of for so long; I would not even be allowed into a military band. I had really enjoyed Army Cadets, and now I would lose this sense of belonging and purpose and my plans for the future had been shattered. Here was yet another confirmation that I simply wasn't good enough. I had failed miserably, just like I always did.

Following my surgery, I woke up and was violently sick as a reaction to the anaesthetic. I was then stuck in physiotherapy for eighteen months, trying to rectify the bone structure in my feet. I had to wear specialist insoles in my shoes because of a massive 'overpronation'; my feet rolled inwards when I walked and caused shooting pains up my legs. More blows to my self-confidence. My weight was yo-yoing, my binging and purging was playing a major roll in my day to day life, and now I couldn't even master the basics of walking.

As I moved up in to year eight, I started cleaning the neighbours' cars and babysitting in the village to get extra money, in order to feed Annie's growing desire for food. I was always so hungry and never felt truly satisfied. It was impossible to fill up what I would describe as permanent void that had taken up residency inside of me. And so, I didn't merely eat, I binged. I ate until my stomach hurt and throbbed with pain.

It was also around this time that I realised just how shrewd I could really be and how I could manipulate things to get what Joanne wanted and Annie needed. I worked out the fashionable trends at school, particularly what other kids collected. I would then buy those things such as stickers, albums or magazines and re-sell them at up to five times their face value. My biggest return was on a packet of cigarettes. I paid just 92 pence for a packet of ten Gold Mark; I sold them for total of £5.80, making me a profit of £4.88 (almost 525% return on my initial outlay). This is where I first met Jennie; I sold her my last cigarette for £1.00.

As we exchanged the cigarette and cash combination, Jennie introduced herself and told me that she was in year seven, the year below me. She asked me if I smoked (I didn't). Jennie then offered me the cigarette I had just sold to her. I sealed my lips tightly around it and inhaled deeply, coughing loudly again and again as she stood there and giggled at me, but I was not going to let this beat me and so I tried again and again until I mastered the task.

Jennie and I became inseparable almost immediately; we found we had so much in common, especially our love of powerful music. For the rest of our lunch break that day we sat talking as if we had known each other our whole lives. By the time the next lesson started, we had agreed to meet each other at lunchtime the following day. Over the next few weeks it became apparent just how alike we really were; she too had issues connecting with her dad (but that is her story to tell not mine). I felt that I had finally met someone who at long last understood what I was going through and how I felt. We shared absolutely everything. I even told Jennie about Annie and with her support, (and finally having someone that understood me) she helped me to control Annie for a little while. Jennie promised me that she would never tell a living soul about Annie, and take it to the grave she did. As our friendship continued to grow, I would call around her house each morning so that we could walk to school together, as well as meeting each other every break time.

During the school holidays, I would spend most of my spare time around at Jennie's house, or she would be at mine. Fairly typically I guess we both enjoyed what the other had. While I longed for the whole stereotypical family unit, consisting of mum and dad and everything that came with that, Jennie relished the emotional side of my family (I only found this out after her death in 2003). While I loved being at her house, with her young fun mum; she would rather be at mine with my 'mumsy' mum, who had nothing financially, but gave everything to her children emotionally.

It was around this time that strange things started to happen to me that I could not explain (I still can't if I am honest). The first weird incident happened in my bedroom during the night: I woke up to hear the sound of the door handle rattling, like someone was twisting it and trying to get in to the bedroom (it was a turn-able old Victorian kind of handle). My sister Kelli was fast asleep in her bed and I was sooooo scared! I pulled the covers up over my head to try and hide. This happened several more times over the next month or so, and then one night the door actually swung open, but there was no one there. I think my mum must have thought at first that I was still acting out, when I ran in her bedroom screaming and crying, but she could see I was genuinely terrified. After this I refused to ever sleep in that room again, so eventually Mum had to move me and

Kelli to her bedroom and she moved in to our old one.

Then the vivid dreams, sleepwalking and talking in my sleep began to plague my nights, which I am told started towards the end of June 1992. One night, I had such a scary and vivid dream - that my granddad had died from prostrate cancer on September 23rd between 00.00 and 01.00. It was a horrible, ghastly dream and I woke from it crying and gasping for breath. Mum told me that I was just having a nightmare and not to worry about it because Granddad was well and there was nothing wrong with him. (She could not understand how real this felt to me until September the 23rd 1994, 00.23am.)

The sleepwalking was embarrassing and potentially dangerous, but it must have been hilarious to witness! During one of these vivid dreams, I was being chased around the local swimming pool, and up onto the third level diving board. In my sleep, I jumped from my top bunk, as I would if I was jumping feet first in to an actual swimming pool (thank God I didn't dive!). I landed on the floor and woke up in agony, having really hurt my already damaged foot. It was at this point Mum decided to split the bunk beds into single beds! Oh some of the places I have woken up too! One February, I was woken up by the realisation that I was freezing; I threw back my duvet to find that I was now dressed in a bikini (I had gone to bed in fleece pyjamas!). But I think the funniest experience though has to be me waking up naked in a wheelbarrow.

August 6ᵗʰ, 1992

What a day. Jennie and I continued to enjoy our long summer break, and our friendship had grown stronger and stronger. Unfortunately she hadn't been able to come swimming with me this day because she was on holiday, but I had met up with some other friends to enjoy a new pool (with all the latest slides and waves machines) which had opened up nearby. On the bus ride home there was a terrible, terrible accident.

The bus I was travelling on hit a pedestrian. Getting off the bus, I was greeted by the most horrendous sight, like something that you would imagine in a horror movie. The woman's limbs were contorted in all different directions and everyone around me was just gasping and looking at her as she lay in the middle of the road.

I was just thirteen years old and couldn't understand why no-one was doing anything! Why was no one trying to help her? She was still alive; we could all hear her whimpering in agony. I couldn't stand to watch her lying there all alone and in pain surrounded by people talking but not actually helping, so I walked over to comfort her. While I was sitting on the cold, wet tarmac with her, simply holding her hand and talking to her, trying to reassure her that everything would be OK, she stopped breathing. I must have gone into auto pilot and remembered my first aid training from Army Cadets, because I started Cardiopulmonary Resuscitation (CPR). The first thing I had to do was to pull her false teeth out of her bottom lip, so that I could create a seal around her mouth with mine and then I was breathing in to another human being and doing chest compressions to try and keep her alive. It was so very exhausting (nothing like my training on a rubber doll); those few minutes seemed to take an eternity, before finally the ambulance and police arrived.

Unfortunately, the woman died and I later found out that she had walked out in front of the bus deliberately, leaving her wedding dress and her husband's suit lying on their bed with a suicide letter. She was only middle-aged, but her husband had died earlier in the year and she felt that couldn't live without him. I don't remember how I found out this information (maybe it was from the police interviews that I had to give following the incident), but what I do remember is that I couldn't get the image of her broken body out of my young mind. I could see her face and her lying in the road every time I closed my eyes. Every time I saw or was on a bus I would think about it. I turned fourteen shortly after the accident, and this is when I first started drinking: to blank out these horrifying images.

September, 1992

Jennie and I returned to school; I had moved up to year nine and Jennie was now in year eight. The only thing that either of us was really interested in at school was our music classes, I had carried on playing my trumpet despite giving up Army Cadets, and both of us had joined the school choir. We were natural singers and we escaped in song often over the next few years, through school productions and plays. We also sang outside of the school too, after one of the teachers encouraged us to join a choir in Southwell Minister. This lead to us singing at the Royal Concert Hall and Albert Hall on numerous occasions.

Despite these successes, Jennie and I also brought the worst out in each other. We would arrange to meet during classes for crafty smoke breaks, or we would bunk off from school all together. We would then go to a local hangout known as Witches' Woods. Right in the middle of this wood was an area used by all the local teens, complete with a fire pit and rope swings. When we were there, we would spend our days drinking cheap cider and escaping from the world. Jennie was the first person I ever got drunk with, and also the first person I experimented on drugs with. On one occasion we tried LSD (for anyone who knows how bouncy I am in life now, can you seriously imagine me on acid?!). The things I 'saw' that night were very interesting, to say the least, including flying pink elephants with a green number one on their backs and furry blue creatures jumping out of the stereo speakers in Jennie's house. While I am not proud of some of the things that I have done, it was my way of escaping from my life and for those few and far between moments I no longer hurt or hated myself.

17th December, 1992

I was getting bigger and bigger. When the bullying started, I was at my heaviest of 13 stone 6 pounds, which for a girl of 5 foot 3 ½ inches (yes that half an inch makes all the difference), is *very* large. All the pupils had been called in for a full assembly with the School Governor just before we broke up for the Christmas holidays. This was nothing unusual. However, this time the Head Teacher announced that one of his pupils had brought great credit to the school and that he wanted to read a letter out which he had received that morning. The whole school started whispering to each other; we all wondered who it was and what they had done. Then the Head coughed loudly before booming "Silence please everyone." The whole room fell into total silence; you could have heard a pin drop! Then he began to read the letter:

Dear Mr Gillen.

Re: Joanne Lynn Allott:

Joanne's recent conduct reflects great credit on herself and your school. I recently commended her in open court. Notwithstanding her age, she virtually 'took control' of a situation involving a fatal road traffic accident collision, even though several adults were present and did nothing. She exhibited a degree of maturity way beyond her years and greatly impressed police officers attending the scene.

Young people are often criticised for their attitudes and lack of care. But Joanne has demonstrated that there are young people out there who are prepared to accept responsibility and do what they feel to be right.

Yours sincerely.

Peter Jenkin-Jones.

A different child would have beamed with pride, even if they had been a little uncomfortable with the sudden attention. I had already become so insecure because of my size, that having the whole school gasping, with their eyes fixated on me was intolerable, and there was no means of escape. Mr Gillen then spoke again "Joanne where are you?" I wanted to slide under my chair and hide. I had never asked for any of this attention. Jennie sat next to me smiling and nudging me to get up and to go onto the stage which I finally managed. I reluctantly collected the letter from the Head. Of course, children will be children, and boy can they be unkind. They weren't suddenly keen to be friends with me and I certainly didn't become a hero in their eyes because of my actions. No, instead, the bullying really got in to full swing. It started with snide little comments regarding that assembly and I tried not to let it worry me at first.

February, 1993

By now the taunts had got so bad that I refused to ever take part in a Physical Education class again. The final straw was after a swimming lesson when all the other girls were sniggering about me in my swimming costume while I was in the shower.

Jennie had a confidence that I really admired and she never seemed to worry about my weight, she saw me. When I was upset, she would cuddle me and tell me not to worry about it: "Lard ass? Poppycock, hey I'm known as Torpedo Tits, it's just more of us to love." I wished that I had her attitude, but it was easier for her: she was the beautiful swan, while I was the ugly duckling.

For each PE lesson that I didn't attend, I would go and hide myself away in the music department. Playing my trumpet was a way for me to vent my frustration at the world that I found so very cruel. I had felt like a fraud for so long and harboured so much pain, fear, hate - all of those strong emotions you should never have to feel as a child. I had tried to be something more ordinary and something more acceptable, but (like the ugly duckling) I felt as though I didn't belong.

Believing this allowed me to justify the abuse of myself, my body and my mind; it allowed me to feel something, anything, regardless of how painful that concept is in reality now. It was in those moments of pure emotion that I hated myself the most. Not understood by the outside world, I felt cast-out, embarrassed, different, a fat freak.

January, 1994

I had been hiding myself in the back room of the music department for about a year, practicing and practicing my trumpet until my lips hurt and I could play no more. During this time, the bullying was got worse and worse. It started with name calling by a small group of girls at first, chanting "Fat, Ugly, Useless. Fat, Ugly, Useless." again and again whenever they saw me. I could feel the tears welling up in my eyes, but I didn't want them to see me cry and so I just walked away, sometimes crying and crying in the toilets once I was out of sight.

Then one day I got a letter from a boy at school. He asked me out and told me I had the prettiest eyes he had ever seen. I had never been asked out before, so I was really excited about meeting him. When I arrived at where he had asked me to meet him, the only people waiting for me was the group of girls and some of the local lads. They were all laughing at me "Why would anyone ask want to ask you out?" One of them finally yelled at me across the street. They then proceeded to follow me all the way home, laughing and jeering me. This time I couldn't hold the tears inside and they rolled down my cheeks, fuelling their taunts even more. In the end I screamed at them to leave me alone but this only made them worse; one girl ran up behind me, grabbed my hair and pushed me down to the floor. Then they all ran off laughing with their cruel chants. Until that moment I had not felt the need to binge for about sixteen months, then Annie came back with a vengeance, bringing her friend body dysmorphia to the party. This time, however, I kept Annie a complete secret, even from Jennie.

September 1994

If you hear and see something enough times you cannot help but believe it. This works on both a positive and negative scale. By now, I genuinely believed that if I didn't look attractive then I had nothing and I was nothing. So make myself attractive I would. As I started year ten I had just turned fifteen years old. I decided that I needed plastic surgery to fix all my flaws and I wrote my wish list: a new nose, liposuction and a breast enlargement. Surely these changes would cure all my problems? So I got myself a Saturday job in a shoe shop (earning £15) and worked part time in a supermarket (for £20); a total of £35 per week. I then contacted a plastic surgery group and got some prices:

- £3600 for a new nose
- £3200 for liposuction on my bum and thighs
- £3500 for a breast enlargement.

I worked out that it would take me two hundred and ninety five weeks, if I saved every single penny that I earned, to achieve the £10,600 which I needed. But I swore to myself that I could do this, if I worked really, really hard.

Handel's Minuet and Trio

September 23rd, 1994

I was on a stay over at my friend Josie's house on the night my granddad died. Mum phoned and asked to speak to me in the morning, and as I answered the phone and I was greeted with "Joanne, you need to come home straight away, it's Granddad." My response was "Yes, I know," and I did. I had woken up during the night and turned over to look at the clock. The bright red LCD numbers that were staring back at me read 00.23am and I just *knew* that Granddad had passed away.

October, 1994

Once again, I was venting away in music room number three, avoiding yet another PE lesson. I was so engrossed in the music I was playing, that I hadn't heard the door behind me open. As I finished what I was playing and lowered the instrument to my side, I heard clapping coming from behind me. I turned around to see Mrs Blackwell, one of the music teachers, applauding me. I mean, seriously?! But there she stood, clapping. I didn't know what to do or where to look and felt my face start to get redder and redder. "Joanne! Bravo, bravo! Where on earth does someone your age learn to play Handel with so much passion?" I shrugged my shoulders and dropped my head forward so I was looking at the floor; I didn't know what to say to her. "More importantly," she continued, "Why do I not know you can play so well?" Again I shrugged my shoulders and continued to stare at the floor. "Has the cat got your tongue? Speak to me girl." Finally, I managed a feeble "Practice I guess." That was all I could muster up when it was probably one of the nicest things a teacher had ever said to me. Mrs Blackwell knew me reasonably well, as Jennie and I were in the Choir with her. She even came to our house on choir nights to get changed before we went out to the local church to sing, because she didn't have time to pop home. I suppose it must have been a surprise to her that I had this hidden talent, but I'm not sure I was even aware that I had any real talent until she caught me.

Walking over to me, Mrs Blackwell placed her hand on my right shoulder and asked whether I was having private trumpet lessons (I wasn't, just school lessons) before going on to tell me that I was really very good. She then noticed that I had a piano score with me too, and asked if I would play with her. I have never moved so fast! I gathered my things together and rushed out of the door, feeling like Linford Christie doing the 100 meters in the 1992 Olympics, as I muttered something about needing to get to my next class. I heard her shout for me to wait, but I pretended not to hear her. I wasn't at all used to someone giving me praise and I didn't know what to say, how to act or what to do. So I simply avoided the music department for the rest of that week, hoping that this would all be forgotten about by the time I next had a music lesson.

The following week I attended my music lesson as normal but how wrong I had been: as I walked in through the door, Mrs Blackwell greeted me with "Hi

Joanne, nice to see you again. When you've finished in class I would like you to come to see me in my office please." GULP! There was no getting out of that then. I was convinced that I was in trouble for running away from her the previous week and ignoring her shouting after me, so I just got more and more stressed, worrying for the next hour. I reluctantly went to her office as requested, knocking very gently on the closed door, hoping and praying that she wasn't there or wouldn't hear me.

Mrs Blackwell bellowed for me to come in and then asked me to take a seat as she took off her glasses. I did as I was told and sat down. "Now the reason I wanted to talk to you: the school production is coming up shortly and I would like you to take part and play Minuet and Trio with me. What do you think?" What did I think?! "No way, Miss, I can't." "What do you mean, you can't? Yes you can, and very well may I add." My mind was racing, how would I be able to get myself out of this? I tried to argue that I wasn't good enough, but Mrs Blackwell reminded me that she had heard me play. I could usually be so quick to think on my feet, but suddenly my mind was blank: there was nothing but a tumble weed bouncing around the empty space in my head.

It got worse. Mrs Blackwell then spotted that I had my trumpet with me! Following her reluctantly, I was lead into one of the music rooms where she sat herself down at a piano. "Get your stand up girl, I have not got all day you know!" I got everything together as instructed, but I was nervous as hell inside and shaking like a leaf, despite being told to relax and pretend she wasn't there! Yeah, right, as if that's easy. She began to play the introduction and although I was very familiar with it, I was so scared that I missed my cue. "Miss, I told you that I couldn't do it." "Couldn't / can't do not exist in music Joanne, let's take it from the top. Just take a deep breath and compose yourself." I breathed in deeply and this time I did manage to start and to play through to the end. Though not perfect, it was from start to finish none the less. "Joanne, see, what did I tell you? I knew you could do it! A little bit of fine tweaking and it will be absolutely great!" Mrs Blackwell enthused, smiling at me! "Do you have a metronome?" I didn't. I also knew that Mum wouldn't be able to afford one for me. Mrs Blackwell must have picked up on my uncomfortable body language and instantly offered to lend me hers so that I could practice and get my timings 'absolutely spot on'. It was such a nice simple thing for her to do, but all that I could think about was how am I was going to get myself out of this . . .

As the weeks went past I would spend hours practicing Handel's Minuet and Trio, because I didn't want to let Mrs Blackwell down when she had so much faith in me. Unfortunately, I didn't have a mute which I really needed to be able to practice at home properly. It is such a loud and passionate piece of music that it would disturb the neighbours in our row of terraced houses. My mum, thinking on her feet, got hold of an old industrial cotton reel from work which acted somewhat as a substitute mute for me, reducing the volume slightly when I put it in the bell. I also found that if I played into my wardrobe full of clothes this reduced the noise a little more. Obviously this was far from the ideal, so most of my proper practice was done at school. I sacrificed every lunch break for weeks and weeks as well as practicing two or three times a week with Mrs Blackwell, so that I could get used to playing alongside a piano. As we spent more time together, I started to call Mrs Blackwell by her first name, Joy, and I grew to really appreciate the belief she had in me. I now knew I could do it, and the more I practiced the more confident I became. Then the night before the concert it dawned on me, I would be centre of the stage, centre of attention, well out of my comfort zone, and in full view of everyone; what a nightmare and what if I messed this up? I would be an even bigger laughing stock than I already was.

I barely slept a wink all night worrying about what could go wrong. The following morning I ran up to the music department as fast as I could, knowing I needed to get out of this commitment somehow. "Miss, I can't do it, I don't want to do it, please don't make me do it!" I blurted out at 600 miles an hour, I hadn't even said hello when I ran into her office. "Calm down, will you, you will be absolutely fine, you're just experiencing a little stage fright, that's all." I wasn't convinced, and continued to argue. Joy stood up from her desk, taking a deep breath while shaking her head. She picked up my trumpet and instructed me to follow her. I did as I was told and we went down to the empty school theatre, where she made me set up and play the piece with her to an empty audience. "See that wasn't so bad now, was is it?" And it wasn't. She walked over to me and gave me a reassuring squeeze on the shoulder. Without saying another word, she was saying to me

"Joanne, I know you can do it," and, strangely, I believed her.

November 30th, 1994

I walked out on to the stage that night feeling as confident as I could, although being the last act on hadn't helped my nerves. As I stood looking into the audience as my solo was introduced, I spotted my worst nightmare and saw them sat out there mouthing at me. "Fat, Ugly, Useless; Fat, Ugly, Useless." Over and over again, while pointing at me. The piano introduction started and I willed myself to do the best I that could. I had practiced this piece of music so hard for weeks and weeks, I knew it inside out, upside down and back to front. But I missed the opening introduction and that was it - I knew that I was screwed. I had done everything I knew I would, I had screwed this up, just like I always screwed everything up. Why couldn't I just do something well for once in my life? Why did everything *always* have to go wrong for me, even when I had worked so very hard so that it was just perfect. All those wasted hours and that hard work for nothing! Joy coughed and then played the intro again in such a way it didn't look as though I had missed it, I could see her smiling at me over the top of the piano, almost as if she was shouting with her eyes, "Joanne, come on you can do it, just relax and play with all the passion I know you have!" The light was blinding me, but all I could still see was *them*, sniggering and pointing at me! The adrenaline and fear was pulsing through my veins as the blood was pumping around my body. I inhaled deeply and then blew out – I was an octave out, I really *had* messed up. I knew it, and so did the audience.

As I ran from the stage, all I could hear was laughing. I didn't even stop to grab the rest of my belongings, I felt so stupid that I just wanted to get home as quickly as I could. It was a dark and wet November night and my house was over a three mile walk from school, but I didn't care, I wasn't thinking straight. Ten minutes or so into my walk home, a car slowed down at the side of me. Joy wound her window down and asked me to get in the car "NO! This is all your fault, I told you I couldn't do it, but you made me, you made me and I made myself look stupid in front of everyone," I screamed. She got out of the car and after more arguing, I gave in to her reasoning that it was too cold and damp to be walking home without a coat. "What on earth happened to you out there?" She asked. I didn't answer her and sat there in silence just looking out of the car window and counting the street lights as we passed them to drown out the questions she was asking me, and to keep myself distracted from answering them. "I saw your face change. You saw someone out in the audience, didn't you? What's going on? Are you being bullied?" (And there we have a winner!) "Miss, it doesn't matter." I simply replied, ignoring her pleas to let her help me and grateful that we were at the end of my street and I could end the questioning. I told her I could walk from here.

The following day I was in my English lesson when Joy knocked on the door and approached my English teacher; they both looked up at me before she came over to me and asked me to follow her. Reluctantly, I did as I was told and followed her to her office in the music department. As she closed the door behind me, Joy continued the conversation from the night before, telling me with a pitying look in her eyes that she only wanted to help me. As I started to cry she handed me some tissues and spoke so gently and with genuine kindness, asking me again to tell her what the problem was. I tried to convince her I was fine, but somehow I knew she wasn't going to let this go, and so eventually I told her the truth. Well, most of it. "I am being bullied, but please don't ask me to tell you who it is, because I won't, it will only make things far worse for me!"

Joy didn't pressure me for any further details, and I was relieved although a little surprised. I was even more surprised by what she said once I had composed myself. "Joanne, I want you back up on that stage tonight, do you hear me?" I looked at her dead in the eye and I could see that she was serious! "No way Miss, I'm really sorry but I can't, absolutely no way!" I have no idea how she managed to convince me to do it (something about facing your fears and getting back on the horse you've fallen from), because I was so determined that I was never going to get back up there. After the night before, there was no way would I ever make a fool of myself like that again! But manage to convince me she did. I'm so glad that I did get back up there that night, because this time I played the piece phenomenally, receiving a standing ovation from the entire audience. I couldn't believe it, I did it, I really *did it*.

Joy gave me a lift home following the concert and congratulated me on doing so well. She then re-broached the subject of my bullying again, telling me that I should tell my mum. I rolled my eyes and argued that there was no point upsetting and worrying Mum when I only had six months left at school anyway; "I can cope with it on my own. I have for a long time!" There was an awkward silence and then "Joanne that is the problem: you shouldn't have to cope on your own at your age. I'm a mum myself, and I would want to know if my son was going through this. Don't you think your mum would be upset, if she found out that you had been dealing with this all on your own and that she hadn't been there to help you?"

How could I argue with that? "Yes, but, but, but . . ." I couldn't think of anything else to say or add. Joy then said she would come in with me while I told my mum, "She is a lovely lady." I knew she wasn't going to let me get out of this one. Of course, it was the right thing to do, but I was more concerned about my mum worrying about me, than I was about what was actually happening to me. "It is only name-calling and there was the one push. I shouldn't be so sensitive, I should just ignore it." I argued as we turned into my street. She pulled the up car right outside my house and started to get out. Now I knew she was serious. "It doesn't matter what it is, no one has the right to upset or hurt you, it's still bullying!"

Mum greeted us both, but looked at me oddly, as if to ask what I had been up to, as she hadn't been expecting to see Joy. They exchanged pleasantries before Joy said "I'm fine Sue, but Joanne has something she needs to tell you." Mum threw her eyes in my direction before asking "What have you been up to then, Madame?" This was exactly why I didn't want to talk to her. I can't really say I blamed her because I had, so far, been a far from perfect daughter, she knew all about my smoking and drinking. Looking back now, I realise a lot of this was just the normal teenage rebellion stuff and I guess my friends were doing the same or worse, but obviously Mum didn't know my own reasons for this behaviour. She had no idea how unhappy I really was inside. No one did except me, because I was so very good at hiding my feelings and wearing my happy face mask!

My mum was actually a pretty cool mum, looking back on it now; I know most of my friends thought so. She used to allow us to have a drink, in moderation, at the weekends. She would allow me to have a friend over, like Jennie (with her parent's permission of course) and would even get the drink in for us. Jennie and I both looked and acted much older than we were, and we even used to go out clubbing with Jennie's mum. Now I know some people may read that and be shocked, because we were only fifteen, but when I look back at this now, I know the reason they did this was because they were in control, they knew what we were up to and exactly what, and how much, we were drinking. Most importantly, they knew that we were safer under their supervision than outside of it, so rather than us doing this behind their backs on some park bench or somewhere, they allowed us to do it in a controlled and supervised environment.

Everyone outside of my house thought I was Little Miss Perfect, because I acted like the blue eyed girl, but behind closed doors I was far from it. I was in so much pain deep inside myself that I acted out at home towards both my mum and sister. I guess this is why I felt it was easier just to deal with issues on my own, because I knew my mum already had enough on her plate dealing with me; she didn't need any more problems as well. But I didn't have any choice this time; I had no option but to tell her the truth about being bullied. I don't know why I have never found it easy to talk to people, maybe it's because I didn't want to bother or upset anyone and all I ever really wanted was a normal, simple life. So I created this happy, bubbly exterior persona to protect myself and to hide behind, and if I didn't let anyone in, I couldn't get any more hurt than I already was. Doing this, I think I thought I would be safer.

December, 1994

Three weeks later, it was the end of term for the Christmas break and I couldn't wait to get out of school for a while. I only had two more terms left and then I would be done for good; I couldn't wait to leave school, because I hated everything about the place. I got home from school and emptied my school bag, as I always did. Only this time, inside it, I found a small square envelope which I opened with some trepidation. It was a Christmas card from Joy, thanking me for one of the best school concerts that she had ever done. I was a little surprised by this, but it did make me smile, as I remembered back to a few weeks before and how different each of the nights had been, but I was smiling mainly because Joy had had faith in me, and even though she had pushed me to get back out there, I was really glad she did and was so pleased that she never lost her faith that I could actually pull it off.

January, 1995

Returning to school, I was full of mixed emotions, but I was glad it wasn't too much longer before I could leave school for good. By this time Jennie and I had started to distance a little because she now had a boyfriend. We were still very close, but we saw less of each other than we once did. Most of my time out of school was now spent with my friend Josie. In school, the bullying continued and, in fact, got worse, resulting in me becoming involved in physical fights. My sister was being bullied too now, and while I couldn't or wouldn't defend myself (thinking I was only getting what I deserved), I wasn't going to let anyone hurt Kelli. Mum eventually moved Kelli to another school to prevent her going though what I had been though, but it was too late for me. If I bothered to attend school at all now, most of my day I would hide away in the music department. Joy gave me little jobs to keep me amused and busy; in honesty I think all the other teachers had given up on me, but not Joy.

One day, she finally asked about my plans for when I left school. As I shrugged my shoulders saying I just wanted to get a job, any job (I was just delighted to be leaving), Joy raised her voice at me for the first time. "Joanne, you are so smart, but so unwilling to be so, why do you push against what others fight to have?" How does a fifteen year old answer that? "Erm, let me see, my self esteem is so low that I would rather not face the inevitable failure that awaits me, so instead I simply do nothing?" Or perhaps "I am so afraid to be at home because my family think I'm the devil incarnate and they don't understand me." Instead, I just stood in silence staring at Joy until she gestured for me to leave. I turned and walked out of the door.

One by one my exams came and went. If I bothered to attend, all I did was to put my name on the paper, get up and walk out of the exam room. The only two exams I finished were Maths and Music (which happened to be my last exam). Once I finished that, I went to say my goodbye to the only teacher who had ever shown any kind of interest in me or tried to help me.

I knocked on Joy's door, which was semi ajar. "Miss, I just wanted to say thank you for everything and for trying to help me." She asked me to come in, take a seat and explained that she had just taken over a ladies' choir which was to meet on Monday nights at the school. Did I want to join and continue with my music? As she was talking, Joy went in to her top drawer and pulled out a small gift-wrapped package. "This is a thank you for all the hard work you have done around here for me." I didn't know what to say, and again just sat staring at her in silence. She placed the small package in to my hands. "Thank you Miss." "You're welcome Joanne. Now go home and have a great summer, and don't forget to let me know about the singing." I waited until I got home to un-wrap the parcel because I was too embarrassed to open it in front of Joy. My gift was a pretty note book and inside there was a card which said. "Dear Joanne, Thank you for all your help within the music department and being the chief chorister of the choir over the past year. Olive, AKA Joy Blackwell."

A Pair of Socks and a Bag of Chips

May, 1995

It had been several months now since I had left school. I knew that I needed to get a full time job but initially I choose to bum around while I decided what it was that I wanted to do. I still had my Saturday job and part time job on the fruit and vegetable stall, but I wasn't doing anything to find full time work. Part of me hung onto what Joy had said about me being smart, while the ever growing pessimist in me drop-kicked that notion straight back to the floor. Finally, I decided to take action, and got a full time job working as a factory machinist in the little village where I lived. I lasted a whole two days before walking out because I hated it. I then got another similar job in the next town, but again didn't last very long (about two weeks) before I decided that being a factory machinist was definitely not the right job for me. Having spent a few weeks looking in the Job Centre on a daily basis, I signed up with a temping agency for some kind of office-based work, thinking I would be more suited to that. I also felt more comfortable going for temporary jobs: if I didn't have commit to something permanent, then I wouldn't be a failure again when it didn't work out.

As the summer progressed, I was drinking far too much; more than anyone knew and sometimes in secret. I needed the drink as a way to escape how I was feeling inside. I would look in the mirror and all I could see was this fat ugly young woman staring back at me. I felt sick looking at her and yet I kept on looking. I would constantly analyse my body in front of the full length mirror I had in my bedroom, pinching at my rolls of fat. My favourite question, for the next fifteen years became "Does my bum look big in this?" I know used to drive my friends and family nuts with this question. I would sometimes walk into the lounge to be greeted by "No!" from Mum or Kelli, before the question had even escaped my mouth!

And so, I drank, because when I wasn't sober I could become the confident person that I longed to be. I had become a very good actress, masking my problems so well that no one knew how I was really feeling inside. I also became a real practical joker. I was such fun, such a laugh, but deep inside I felt lonely, miserable and isolated. I couldn't shake the feeling that I didn't belong. The more successful my persona was, the more the real Joanne didn't fit.

Annie was also now in full destruction mode and I was binging in secret anything up to ten times a day. Achieving this while living with my mum and Kelli was no mean feat. I *was* clever, even if I didn't appreciate it at the time; I had plenty of tricks up my sleeve and became more and more sneaky and deceitful. I rarely used the bathroom at home because I knew if I started going there each time I needed to purge, I would draw too much attention to myself. Instead, when anyone else was at home, I would pretend to listen to music in my bedroom and then block the door so that I could throw up into carrier bags. I would hide these bags all around my bedroom (I'm amazed the smell didn't give me away). I would then sneak the bags out of the house in my shoulder bag. Often, I would get up in the middle of the night and pretend to go to the bathroom. My detour would take me outside, beyond our own dustbins and to one of the neighbour's. We lived in a row of eight terraced houses; this was so easy to get away with. On other occasions, I would ask my mum if she needed anything from the shops so that I had an excuse to get out of the house. Any excuse you can think of, so that I could find some privacy and purge, believe me I used them all! I was trapped in a vicious circle of destruction. I was still desperate to have plastic surgery, believing that this would make me beautiful and solve my problems, but in the mean time I was spending instead of saving, either on food for Annie or on alcohol for Joanne's escapes from reality.

August, 1995

Having had little joy at work, I thought about going to college, convinced that it would be something different, and *had* be better than school. I started an NVQ in Leisure and Tourism at West Nott's College; again lasting only a matter of weeks. This time, I didn't actually want to leave, and was really enjoying the course, but I couldn't afford to fund my partying or Annie's binges any longer. I quit, once again, to avoid the inevitable failure that waited ahead. Mum must have been so frustrated with me; the only thing I did stick to was my singing on Monday nights. I remember Joy once questioning me about my eating habits, after a choir rehearsal one Monday evening, because I had lost so much weight in the six months since leaving school. I just talked my way out of it, saying it must have been puppy fat and now I was eating sensibly and working out; so I was able to continue on with my self destruction.

My mum finally arranged an interview for me at the sock factory where she worked. I got the job and was placed on the tagging section on piece rate, with a minimum wage back up. Simply put I had the potential to earn good money if I put the effort in, or I could do less and take the minimum wage home. A few weeks after starting this job, I was in the bathroom washing my hands and I had a really strange feeling: like when you shudder and say 'someone just walked over my grave'. I looked up in to the mirror and saw that standing behind me was a middle aged lady smiling. I assumed she was the factory cleaner or another employee that I hadn't met yet, so I just politely smiled back and continued to wash my hands. I looked up again before moving over to the hand drier and she was still in exactly the same position with the exact same smile on her face, so I turned around to ask her if everything was OK. As I did this, I looked her up and down. When I noticed she had no feet I spun around faster than I had ever moved in my life and ran back to my work station, not believing what my eyes had told me.

When I got back to my bench, a couple of the other women asked me if I was OK and I reassured them that I was fine. One girl then piped up "Joanne, are you sure you're OK? You look like you've just seen a ghost!" When I said I thought that I had and explained, as requested, what I had seen, needless to say they all burst out laughing. I knew what I had seen, but in the end I backed down, saying "OK, whatever," and I went along with their joke at my expense. I learnt a very valuable lesson from this about keeping my mouth shut in future. A few days later a friend of my mum's approached me, asking about my 'incident' in the Ladies'. I rolled my eyes saying "Margaret, just leave it, *please.* I've learnt my lesson. Maybe I was over-tired or something." She grabbed my arm "Joanne, please just tell me what you saw!" I laughed at her "OK, I saw a little old lady smiling at me in the mirror, she was bright Pink with Green spots, hey maybe she was Mr Blobby's Mum! What do you think?" Margaret pressed on asking me to please tell her what I had seen and whether there was anything unusual about it. I sighed, and explained that I had thought that I was looking at a normal person until the moment that I noticed the missing feet, but now I thought she must be a ghost "Go on, now you take the piss too." Margaret looked at me and smiled "I believe you. I think you saw Aggie the factory spook. I have worked here years and several people have seen her; each saying the same thing about her having no feet! She died on a train line that used to run where the factory now stands and apparently she lost her feet in the accident. Loads of people claim to have smelt her but only a handful have seen her!" I really thought that I was going to pass out as Margaret told me this. I had begun to doubt what I had actually seen myself, particularly because 'Aggie' didn't fit the stereotype of a ghost like you see at the movies, being transparent and vanishing in front of your eyes. The woman I had seen looked just like you and me (minus the feet of course).

May 1996

I had developed a small circle of friends; I worked hard, but boy, I partied harder! Thanks to Annie, I had dropped to nine stone, but I still wasn't happy. I still didn't have the money for the surgery I wanted; I was still eating and drinking it as quickly as I could earn it. So I took another job in a chip shop four evenings a week and worked more hours in the factory to boost my income and bring me closer to the surgery. Then I realised that driving lessons would increase my independence and so these began to eat into my surgery money as well.

April, 1997

I passed my driving test and bought myself a little red Metro instead of a new body. I loved the freedom the car gave me, and I'm sure to the outside world Joanne was doing what normal young women did, but on the inside I was something that I hated. I know hate is a strong word to use in relation to anyone, let alone yourself, but hate myself I did.

Through the choir, my friendship with Joy had continued to grow and once I passed my driving test I started picking up her son from school on Friday afternoons, because I only worked a half day on Fridays. I had always wanted to learn to play the piano, so we agreed that Joy would give me lesson every Friday in return. The lessons lasted for a few weeks, because before long these Friday afternoons became shopping trips or glasses of wine in the garden, a good old gossip and catch up. Despite our age difference Joy became, and has remained, one of my dearest friends.

In the 1980s, there was a girls' game called Fashion Wheel, where you could mix different combinations of heads (with hats and jewellery), middles (tops/blouses etc) and bottoms (trousers or skirts). I was like Fashion Wheel gone wrong, or maybe a couple of leftover bits that no one wanted, but which had been clipped together nonetheless. I was a tiny size 6/8 on top and size 14/16 around the bottom. I was massively, and *very* self-consciously, out of proportion. I used to laugh off the comments I received, but each time someone said something, Annie grew a little stronger. I was *so* obsessive about being the perfect size and shape that I by now I was weighing myself constantly. I would ~~jump~~ *tip toe* onto the scales every morning *and* after each binge *and* before bed *and* in the middle of the night, if I got up then. I was consumed with an image of perfection, except I wasn't trying to be perfect; I just wanted to be normal and my idea of normal was what Annie was striving so hard to achieve. I needed it, I craved it, I had to make myself normal.

September, 1998

I finally visited a plastic surgery group not long after my twentieth birthday, when I probably should have been out enjoying myself with other, far more everyday and inconsequential worries.

My appointment was in a very grand building in Nottingham, almost like a stately home. I had booked to talk to a surgeon about having my breasts enlarged. Being so pear shaped, it seemed logical that if I made my bust bigger there would be a better sense of balance and proportion. I was full of mixed emotions as I waited. What would the surgeon say? What would my new breasts look like? Would it hurt? Would they operate on someone my age? It was only then that I realised I had made this decision without really knowing much about cosmetic surgery at all.

At 14.30 precisely, the receptionist shouted my name and showed me through to the consultation room. The surgeon stood up from a desk in the middle of the room as I entered, extending his hand. He introduced himself and indicated that I should sit down. I remember clearly that I was wearing a tight white T-shirt, with a long flowing orange hippy skirt to hide my bottom half away. "So, Joanne, what can I do for you?" he asked. When I explained that I wanted to get my breasts enlarged, he looked quite concerned and asked why someone so young would want this major surgery. "I'm out of proportion, Doctor! I am much bigger around the bottom half than I am around the top and I want to even this out!" He nodded slowly before asking if I was aware of all the risks involved with this operation. Before he had even finished that sentence, I had heard Annie's voice "Pay attention and keep it together. We've got this. Lie! Lie to him! Lie!" So of course I said yes, and that I had wanted the operation for a very long time. In fact, I wasn't at all aware of the risks involved but neither did I care; all I wanted was to cross this goal off that wish list I had written at the tender age of fifteen; the risks involved were completely insignificant compared to my need to look good.

The surgeon made notes as I was talking and I was just grateful that he didn't know what was going on in my head. I was stupidly surprised when he asked me to go behind a screen and remove the top half of my clothing. I hadn't even given enough thought to the whole thing to realise that was something I might have to do! I was still a virgin and no man had ever seen me naked. When I questioned whether it was necessary, the doctor explained in a very matter-of-fact way that it was the only way he could examine me and take pictures. Pictures?! "Joanne, have you really thought this through?" He went on to explain that he would have to examine me to see if I was a suitable candidate for implants and to take photos so I could see the before and after. "Once I have the pictures today, I can put them onto the computer to give you an idea of the kind of results that could be achieved. OK?" I muttered OK, but I'm not sure he heard me as my heart was beating incredibly loudly as I walked behind the curtain.

I did as I was told; removing my T-shirt and bra and letting him know when I was ready. Of course, I was far from ready, but I would do what I had to do to get what I wanted. The surgeon came around the curtain armed with a camera and a black marker pen and began drawing on my chest and snapping away without a care in the world. After what felt like the longest few minutes of my life, he casually told me he was finished, that I could wipe the pen marks off with some wet wipes, get dressed and join him again at his desk.

Having put myself through such embarrassment, I wasn't prepared for him to say that he didn't think I needed to have my breasts enlarged! "Hear me out, Joanne," he continued when I started to argue. "I have been doing this for a very long time, and even with your skirt on I can see that you are much bigger around you lower half than on top. A breast enlargement can only go so far in achieving the balance you are looking for. Do you do any exercise?" I lied to him again and told him that I trained all the time but just couldn't seem to shift the weight from that area no matter what I did. Of course in reality I hadn't done any exercise since I had been teased in the shower after swimming and had started to avoid PE.

I hoped and prayed that he would believe me. "Well then," he said "My professional advice to you would be to have liposuction." He didn't need to say it twice; liposuction had been on my wish list as well anyway! "OK, if that's what you think!" Unfortunately, that meant I had to 'hop behind the curtain' again to show him my 'problem areas'. He returned with his trusted black marker pen and camera combination. As he drew away on my skin, I was imagining how much better I would look and how much more beautiful I would be once this was all done. I got dressed and took a seat at his desk again. The surgeon then connected the camera to his computer and downloaded the pictures he had just taken. As they appeared, I remember feeling sick: I was humongous. As he started pointing to the areas he felt he could best work with and began pressing the buttons on his mouse, the pictures started to change in front of me. Quite literally the fat was vanishing before my very eyes! I was sold at that point, no matter what the cost, because being slim equalled being beautiful in my eyes and that was worth any amount of money to me!

The surgeon explained to me that he felt he could achieve the best results by working on my bottom, my inner and outer thighs and also on my knees. When I asked what the cost would be, I was told £1,500 *per area*! Now I started to worry. I couldn't afford that, but I really wanted to do it, no matter what. He went on to explain that if I had everything done at the same time, it would be £1,500 for the first area, but as I would be already sedated or asleep, it would only be £500 per area after that, "So a total of £3,000, plus £250 for the hospital bed." "That's fine Doctor!" I excitedly responded, "But I don't want to be put to sleep, unless I have to?" "Why would you not want to be put under? It's not very often someone states that so forcefully!" "The last time I was put to sleep, the anaesthetic made me very ill and I would rather not go through that again." He said OK, and then asked if I needed to hear about their finance options (I didn't) and with that I was booked in for surgery three weeks later.

Those three weeks dragged by so very slowly. Every day I looked in the mirror imagining what I would look like following the surgery, wondering how much more beautiful I would be when I was finally slim. Finally the date arrived and my sister drove me to Altringham for the operation that I was sure would change my life.

October 5th, 1998

We left home at about 6am as my surgery was scheduled for later that morning. As we drove through the Peak District, Kelli asked me if I was scared, bizarrely I wasn't, not even a tiny bit. All that mattered was that I would be thinner. I had been told to wear comfortable, loose trousers and to bring a cushion to sit on for the journey home later that same day. I wore White jogging pants that I had bought specially for the occasion. We arrived just before 9am, with my operation scheduled for 11am. But first, I had to be checked in and sign all the consent forms. Everyone was very nice and the building was beautiful and very classy. I remember looking around thinking "Really? This is a hospital?" Once all the paperwork was completed, I was taken through to a room with four beds in it.

There was a girl in the bed opposite mine, but the other two remained empty until later in the afternoon. The girl introduced herself as Debbie and asked what I was getting done. I was so excited that I didn't mind who knew, so I told her without hesitation, and then asked her what she was having done. "Oh, my nose, an eye-bag removal and some 'lipo' on my double chin." Was her reply. I was really puzzled, because I couldn't see anything wrong with her and didn't think she needed any of those things doing. (Of course, the irony of this didn't occur to me until many years later.) Debbie was scheduled to be the first for surgery that day and they came to fetch her at about 10am. I wished her luck, and she said she'd see me in a while when she had a 'new face'. I was happily chatting away to Kelli, not thinking

70

about my own operation, when I became aware of strange noises coming from the next room. I'm sure the colour drained from my face, Kelli stopped talking and asked if I was feeling OK. "Can you hear that noise?" I responded, "That banging, it sounds like . . . a . . . hammer . . . hitting . . . a . . . chisel!" As I ended the sentence, I knew exactly what I was listening to. That was Debbie's nose job in progress. At that moment I became absolutely terrified of just what awaited me inside that room.

Now, a big part of me wanted to get out of that bed and run away as fast as I could but Kelli told me I was being stupid when I said this. "Don't worry, you'll be asleep and won't feel a thing." I looked at her "But they're not putting me to sleep!" "What the fuck, Joanne?" "I was so scared of not waking up or feeling ill like I did after my foot operation that I asked just to be sedated!" Kelli told me in no uncertain terms that I was nuts. At around 11am, a nurse came though and told me that my operation would be a little late as the surgeon was running over on his last surgery. Debbie was wheeled back on to the ward at 11.15 and the curtains were drawn around her bed. I could hear her wincing in pain. Kelli saw my face and gave my hand a gentle squeeze, "You don't have to do this if you don't want to, Joanne." I pulled my hand away; telling me not to do something was like holding a red flag to a bull in a china shop! "I'm fine!" I snapped back, although I was anything but, if honest. In fact, I was shitting myself.

My surgeon appeared at 11.45, armed with his faithful black marker. "Morning Joanne, are you all ready? I just need to mark you up. Please remove your gown and lie on your stomach." I could feel him drawing over my body, and at this point my heart was in my mouth and I was beginning to feel very sick. He asked me if I had any questions and I finally asked the questions that I should have thought to ask at the original appointment: "Will I feel what you're doing? How much will it hurt afterwards?" He reassured me that this was a 'simple wet procedure' (not the most comforting words I've ever heard!), that I would be given a strong sedative and that I probably wouldn't remember a thing. They would then inject each area with a local anaesthetic so I wouldn't feel anything. Once the anaesthetic had taken effect, he would make ten incisions, which he had just marked up, and then blow me up with water like a balloon. He would then insert the cannula which would send out a high frequency electrical current to melt the fat cells, which would then be sucked out. I wondered how on earth I could have got this far without really knowing what was involved, and whether the water / electrical combination was at all dangerous, but it was too late now! I walked to the theatre, climbed onto the bed and was given an injection in the back of my hand. I remember feeling woozy and light headed and then . . . I was waking up back on the ward, and I was cold, so VERY cold. I pressed my buzzer for the nurse who told me this was a normal reaction and switched on a heater, under my blanket at the bottom of the bed. I asked if everything had gone OK and was told that everything was fine and that I should get some rest and she would return in a little while with something for me to eat. When I woke up again, Kelli was sitting next to me on the edge of the bed. She smiled and asked how I was feeling. I said I was OK, that it didn't really hurt and that I would like to know when I could go home. Kelli disappeared to find nurses' station.

The nurse came back with her and asked how I was feeling, and how I would rate my discomfort on a scale of one to ten. I told her about three; I felt like I'd had a bad fall and was bruised, but that was all. "That's good to hear, but a little unexpected; maybe you have a very high pain threshold or perhaps the anaesthetic hasn't fully worn off yet." That didn't bode well. She lifted up the blanket to check on me. "Not much water there. Mind you, that's hardly surprising!" I was confused and asked her what she meant. "Joanne, you are a very stubborn young lady! We tried to get you into a wheelchair to bring you back to your bed. You refused point blank, stating that you were not an invalid and you would walk. Because liposuction is a wet procedure, there is still water under the surface of the skin. That's why you felt so cold, we put pads under you in the bed to absorb the water, but when you insisted on walking, I had to walk behind you with a mop – that's the first time that's ever happened to me!" I smiled and apologised as Kelli giggled! "That's Joanne for you alright; she never does anything she's told!" I just gave her the death stare, which meant 'shut up'.

I was told that I would be allowed to go home once the doctor had been to see me. He finally arrived about 3pm. "Well Joanne, we got some pretty good results, in fact some of the best results I've had for a while, we managed to get four litres of fat out of you." I thought about this for a minute, then I realised just how much that was (two two-litre coke bottles!) my face must have lit up the place. He asked me to turn over so he could examine me. "OK, once you have eaten something, we'll get that pressure garment on and you can go home, how does that sound?" It sounded great to me; I was very hungry and keen to go home. I was put into my pressure garment about 15.30, before I was discharged. The pressure garments were like a pair of spandex pants which were crutchless; very attractive – NOT! I was given a list of instructions about how to take care of myself and what to do to get the best results from my surgery.

I'm convinced Kelli got her revenge for all those times I was mean to her as a child during the drive home that afternoon. I am sure she intentionally aimed for every pot hole that she could find! Because boy, *now* I was in pain like I had never felt in my life. It was only at this point that it began to dawn on me just what I had put myself through, and all to be thin. Thankfully, the excruciating pain only lasted for the first night and then became a dull ache which was nothing I couldn't cope with. This ache lasted for about two weeks, but I just got on with it and only had two days off work instead of the two weeks that had been recommended. I did everything that the surgeon had told me to do for a few weeks and then it was time to go back to get my stitches removed and for my first check up. I was still badly bruised, which I expected, but I was also concerned that my right bum cheek looked bigger than my left! I was reassured that this was quite normal and that different parts of my body would swell and recover at different rates. I wasn't convinced, but assumed they knew more about liposuction than I did.

My next check up appointment was scheduled for three months later. Every day I would look at myself and take measurements (so much for becoming *less* obsessed with my body!) I was waiting for the magical miracle that I had seen on the surgeon's computer during my initial consultation. Of course, the miracle transformation never materialised. I was young and naïve, I hadn't thought about the pain or the wait for results and I'd assumed that it would be instantaneous. Unfortunately, the only thing that was obvious, almost four months after my surgery was that I had been right about my bum cheeks being different sizes. I am not talking about a subtle difference either! Heading back to the clinic, I didn't even let the surgeon greet me before I blurted out "Doctor, I *do* have one side bigger than the other!" He examined me and agreed, saying that it could happen sometimes (I was sure that I hadn't been warned about that, but on the other hand, would I have listened anyway?) "Not to worry," he said "We'll sort that out for you." Two weeks later I was off for liposuction round two! You would think the initial results would have been enough to put me off doing anything like that again, wouldn't you? Ummmmmmm . . .

Plastic Fantastic

After my second round of liposuction, I was a perfect size ten. Was I happy? Of course not! I was still not good enough, still not perfect enough! Every time I achieved a goal that I set myself in regards to the way I looked, I would push it further and need to improve myself some more. So I was still abusing my body and still wrecking my teeth and my oesophagus with the stomach acid from my continual purges. I then bleached my hair as another change, trying anything to be something new, something better than I was.

Summer, 1999

Boy, did I take Prince seriously! I *really* partied like it was 1999! The internal misery continued, but it must have looked to other people as if I was having a fantastic time. Although I didn't like myself, I did like helping other people, and I was keen to do something to mark my 21st birthday. I collected over £350 in sponsorship for a local hospice, to do a parachute jump! Since my school years and my time with the Army Cadets, I had always liked to push myself and take risks. This was the sort of challenge where failure wasn't an option! But I couldn't believe what I was doing, when I was looking out of the plane's window at 10,000 feet! I couldn't do it; I no longer had the confidence to push myself to do extreme things that I once did, and so I backed out at the last minute.

I went Kavos with some friends, to celebrate my twenty first birthday. Whenever I've been able to afford it, I have always booked great holidays and visited different and interesting places. As usual with me, it's a double edged sword – yes, I'm very lucky, and have travelled more than many people have, but it was also a security blanket. If I wasn't at work, I *had* to make sure I was surrounded by friends and if I could escape my day to day life, all the better. Time on my own, time thinking, was something I wanted to avoid at all costs! Perhaps strangely, given my unhealthy relationship with food, I was also developing a love of food, and really enjoyed trying the local cuisine in different countries. *This* particular holiday was one of the craziest I've ever had! It rained so hard that the place flooded, but no way was I going to let that ruin our fun. Joanne the life-and-soul-of-the-party arrived in full force and persuaded everyone to buy lilos, which we were soon racing on – down the main strip and with a beer in each hand! It was great fun when you're twenty one!

When I returned home, I continued working hard in both my jobs, because I still wanted a breast enlargement. My mum knew about this and wasn't happy, but by now she realised that if I wanted something badly enough then I would do it, no matter what she, or anyone else, said or thought. When Mum had tried to talk me out of having liposuction, I had told her in no uncertain terms that it was *my* money and *my* body and I could do what I wanted with them both because I was twenty. Now, I realise she was simply being a normal concerned parent, but of course at the time I thought she was just interfering and that I knew better than she did.

September, 1999

I fell in love for the first time (or thought I did!) I was out with Kelli and her best friend Vicki at Yates's bar in Mansfield one Sunday evening, wearing a red boob tube and skin tight black leather biker trousers. Unusually for me, I was feeling pretty good about myself when, through the crowd, I spotted Chris.

I nudged my sister and pointed him out to her, because she was always trying to fix me up with guys who were just not my type at all. Kelli told me I looked 'hot to trot' and that I should go and talk to him, but I shook my head and went off to the toilet. I was absolutely mortified to see, when I came back out, that Vicki was over talking to him. I ran over to Kelli and told her we had to leave immediately. I may not have had enough confidence to talk to him myself, but your friends approaching some guy you liked was school girl stuff and I wanted the ground to open up and swallow me whole!

I looked up again and saw that he was staring at me. My face went so red I'm not sure if you could see where my embarrassment started and my red top ended. Vicki was heading back our way, so I grabbed Kelli's drink, then Vicki's, and put them on the table. Then I dragged both girls out of the bar! I was furious, and told them never, ever, to do that to me again. Apparently Vicki told me that he thought I was cute, but I wasn't listening. I couldn't 'calm down' as requested, and continued to gripe about them making a complete fool of me.

What I didn't realise was how well they knew me. Vicki had warned Chris that I would completely flip if I saw her talking to him. She'd also told him our pub route! Later that evening, as we sat in the last pub, he and his friend walked in. I wanted to hide under the table or get out of there, because he was heading my way and then Vicki grabbed Kelli and they disappeared into the crowd! Shit! "Hi Joanne, I'm Chris. Would you like a drink?" All I was thinking was how I had really been set up but I had had a few drinks already by now, so I accepted and we spent the rest of the evening chatting. Chris told me he was a sailor who was on a training course nearby for the next week. He was from Burnham on Sea in Somerset, but worked in Scotland and he was thirty eight and divorced with 2 children. I knew my Mum wouldn't be happy about that and I was right; she hit the roof when I told her: "He's probably got a girl in every port! He's too old for you, you're only twenty one and he's thirty eight, that's almost twice your age." She snapped.

That still didn't stop me, and the next week was very intense to say the least. We saw each other each night that week, talking into the early hours. On the Wednesday night, we had been out for a drink and a dance and ended up back at his hotel. Romantically (and physically) I had never been involved with anyone. How could I, with all my insecurities? I was too fat and too ugly; my list of faults went on and on. I was twenty one years old and back at Chris's hotel with no idea what I was doing. I had never slept with anyone and I was terrified of being seen naked. My heart was pounding as Chris leant in gently to kiss my neck, working slowly down to my clavicle. As he began to unbutton my blouse I felt a rise of panic inside me and I pulled away from him. I stood up and backed away. I was trying to re-button my blouse, but I couldn't because I was shaking too hard. Chris smiled at me before standing up and gently clasping my hands to stop them from shaking.

He then began to fasten up the buttons on my blouse, saying "Well, I've never had that effect on anyone before! Joanne, you don't have to be scared; I'm not going to hurt you and you don't have to do anything that you don't want to." With difficulty, I met his eye "It's not that I don't want to . . . I . . . I . . . I . . ." Chris tenderly planted his lips on mine so I didn't have to finish that awkward sentence, he then pushed me tenderly away saying "I know." I was so embarrassed I just grabbed my handbag and my shoes and ran out of the door, calling back to him that I had to go!

When I got home and climbed in to bed I grabbed my phone to send a message of apology for having run away. But there was a text message already waiting for me: "Thank you for a lovely evening. Let me know you got home safely. Can I see you later?" I smiled thoughtfully as I lay my head back on to my pillow. That was very nice of him, because I was sure I wouldn't hear from him again. Unusually my optimism won me over, and I replied "I'm working a double shift tomorrow, how about Friday?" Within seconds I got a reply: "I don't think I can wait that long! But OK, sleep well."

I arranged to pick Chris up on the Friday evening around 7.30pm, so that we could go out for dinner. As I knocked on his hotel door, I realised that I was a little early. Chris opened the door wearing nothing but a towel wrapped around his waist! I apologised and said I'd meet him downstairs but he said not to be silly and to come in. Wow what a body! I couldn't take my eyes off him as he closed the door behind me. Chris turned to face me and gently clasped my face in his hands and kissed me softly on the lips before saying "You look beautiful." Before heading to the bathroom to finish getting dressed. I laughed nervously.

The rest of the evening flew by in no time and at about midnight, with my body tingling from head to toe; I asked Chris if I could stay the night. I smiled when he said of course, if that was what I really wanted, but inside I was terrified of what he would think about my body. Once back at the hotel Chris was very gentle with me. He kissed me while unzipping the back of my dress which he slipped off my shoulders, letting it fall to the floor. I remember asking him to turn off the light, as I didn't want him to see me wearing nothing but my underwear but Chris stepped back and instead of that he just looked at me, before slowly lifting me on to the bed "My God, Joanne you're beautiful, I want to kiss every inch of you." As he began to kiss me working from my lips, down my neck and towards my breasts, I felt an electrifying current running through my body; Chris gently made love to me before I fell asleep in his arms.

MYSELF, ME AND I

The trust I felt toward Chris, for me to have finally lost my virginity, to have allowed someone, other than that surgeon, to have seen me naked and to have actually touched my body was amazing. I was so glad I could spend this time with him before he left the following day to head back up to Scotland. The following week, however, I was brought back down to Earth with a great big bang.

On the Wednesday when I got home from work, my mum handed me a letter which had arrived that morning. I excitedly ripped it out of her hands and ran upstairs to read it. I couldn't believe Chris had written to me; he'd said he would, but I couldn't believe he actually had. I sat on my bed staring at the letter for a while and then opened the envelope to reveal the smart yellow paper inside. "Dear Joanne, thank you for an amazing week. It was really lovely to meet you and I really do like you. You know I have been married and have two young daughters, well, I was surprised such a beautiful young lady would even continue talking to me after I had told her that." And then came the kick in the stomach. "I got so caught up in the moment with you, and the more time I spent with you the harder it got. I need to tell you that I'm in a relationship and have another child, plus my partner had just found out she was pregnant again before I met you! I'm sorry and I know this letter will hurt you, I really never meant to do so, but I had to be honest and tell you!" It was at this point I threw up all over the bedroom floor.

Mum had been right all along! I should have listened. She came up about half an hour later and was great. I handed her the letter and curled up on my bed, with my back to her. She said nothing and gave me no *I told you so*, even though I'm sure she was thinking it; she just climbed onto the bed with me and held me. I went further into my shell after this experience; my confidence had been nonexistent anyway, but now it was in totally in tatters. To make myself feel better I decided I would treat myself . . . to the new breasts that I'd always wanted.

The new millennium, 2000

This time I decided that before I headed back to the clinic, I would write a list of questions to ask the surgeon, and also do some research into the operation. The last time, I had been so very naïve, not knowing what was involved or what to expect. I was concerned about putting silicone implants into my body, because I had heard some horror stories of the damaging side effects that could happen later. I researched online all about breast augmentation, and discovered lots of things I didn't know, like implants being available in not just silicone but also saline, hydro gel (which has since been banned!) and soya oil. I thought about these options and felt that the saline or soya oil would be best for me because if they *did* rupture or leak, these were natural fluids that could be absorbed easily into my body, apparently with minimal side effects. So that was the second decision made (the first being that I wanted to get them done, no matter what!). I then went on to discover that there where different shapes to choose from, including round and tear drop as well as different textures. You could also have temporary or permanent implants; some had a ten year warranty and others less or others more! There were also various ways the operation could be done: under the breast, through the armpit or even by removing your nipples! There was so much to think about.

Finally, I researched all the potential complications and problems. Your breasts could end up different sizes (one experience of being lop-sided was enough, thank you!), you could get an infection after surgery (and your implants may need to be removed to treat this), there could be abnormal scaring around the implant, loss of or over-sensitivity in your nipples, thick red scaring at the entry site and let's not forget the fact that the implants could rupture or leak, which could be fatal! Who knew shopping for a new pair of boobs would be this scary and this complicated? Needless to say, none of this was enough to put me off; all I cared about was how good I would look once they were done. So, armed with my list of questions, I headed back to the clinic.

I had spent so much time at the plastic surgery clinic over the past eighteen months I could have driven there blind-folded and in reverse, and as I walked through the door, Wendy the receptionist (yes, I knew her name!) greeted me and asked what I was getting done this time. When I told her she laughed, saying "I knew you would! I had mine done years ago; one of the best things I ever did!" She then ushered me through to the waiting room and I was called through to see the surgeon a few minutes later. "Hi Joanne, just let me just get your medical notes up." He sat looking at his computer screen and then said "I understand you have come to see me today about getting your breasts enlarged?" "Yes Doctor, I have!" "So what do you know about this procedure?" I gave him the spiel and all the information that I knew; he said he could see that I'd done my homework. He asked if this meant that I knew exactly what I wanted, and told me to tell him so that he could let me know whether it was realistic or not. I told him I would like the soya or saline implants because they were natural, but that I wasn't sure which size or shape would be best and would like to see examples if at all possible. The surgeon reached into his drawer and handed me two implants, one round and one teardrop shaped. "I prefer to work with the round ones, if I am totally honest, Joanne. I will do the teardrop but the results are not as good because they can leave you with a very wide cleavage. When I examine you, I'll tell you what would look best on you." I sat examining the two implants; they were nothing like I imagined they would be. I am not really sure what I had imagined they would look like, but from what I had seen on the internet it wasn't this. They were also much heavier than I'd imagined and the only way to describe what they felt like was thick jelly in a plastic bag.

The Doctor spoke to me again, while I was examining the implants he'd just given to me. "Joanne, you said you would like soya oil or saline implants, is that right?" I agreed. He went back in to his drawer and handed me another implant, but this one was much thinner and had bits of black inside it. I picked it up and asked what it was; it was a saline implant! "And the black bits inside?" "I think that it's mould. That implant has been in my drawer just six months and that's what's happened to it."

When I pulled a face, he continued: "These 'natural' implants are very new on the market. I know the temperature fluctuates in this room, with the heating and weather changes, which could have been what, caused it; I can't say this won't happen inside the body, which also has temperature fluctuations. If you insist on having them I will do them, but I have to make you aware of all the facts I know beforehand."

I put it back on the table and said I had one more question: if I was his daughter, which type of implant would he use and why? He told me he would use a silicone one because although you could find lots of media stories about things going wrong, in fact these cases were very rare and "All you ever hear are the horror stories, never the life changing ones." He went on to explain that he had been a cosmetic surgeon for twenty seven years, working in private clinics and also within the NHS doing reconstructive work. He knew the risks with silicone and what to do should something go wrong. OK, I was convinced. I was soon booked in for surgery six weeks later.

At the time, I was working with two other women, Rachel and Sarah, in the sock factory and we were quite a close knit team. Several weeks before, we'd been swimming together and Rachel had shown us a dimple on top of her breast and asked for our opinion. Sarah and I had both recommended that she had it checked out by her doctor. The dimple had been confirmed as cancerous, and Rachel was now at home recovering from a mastectomy. Sarah and I had arranged to visit her, and I was very concerned about broaching the subject of my forthcoming breast enlargement. On the other hand, I didn't want her to find out any other way, so I felt it best that I was honest with her if she asked me about it (it had been no secret that this was something I had been planning, before she had found out she had cancer). Rachel had, of course, already heard from someone else that I had booked my operation and she made her feelings very clear to me. Whilst I fully understood what she had gone through, and I did explain this to her, I also accepted that she would be annoyed with me, but I hadn't been prepared for just how angry she would be. I didn't let this change my mind, however, and I continued on with my operation, much to Rachel's dismay.

March, 2000

My surgery, unfortunately, didn't go smoothly. This time, my Aunt Sharon had come with me as I required a general anaesthetic, which I was still nervous about, and an over-night stay. Sharon was to stay in a hotel nearby (this was all included in the price). She came with me to the hospital and we had such a giggle while I was waiting to go to theatre. I was being silly, trying all kinds of implant shapes and sizes in a sports bra, while parading around like some kind of a page three model! I finally thought I'd settled for a particular size when the surgeon arrived to speak to me. I had chosen the smallest of the three that he gave me, because they looked huge on my tiny, size eight frame. I was told that they would look smaller when they were inside my body than they did in the sports bra "I always advise people to go the next size up." I said OK, but stressed that I wanted a natural look, "None of this fake 'Jordan' stuck on looking ones for me!" He just smiled and told me I was safe in his hands. I was taken down to the theatre on my bed this time. I told my aunt that I would see her later and waved her goodbye. In the theatre the cannula was put into my hand and I was told to count backwards from ten, I tried fighting against the anaesthetic, but only remember counting back to seven.

I woke up in excruciating pain, like nothing I had ever felt in my life! I called out for the nurse because I couldn't move, not even to get the buzzer. The nurse came over with my surgeon who sat down on the bed and asked the nurse to get him some morphine. I knew at this point it that things were bad. "Joanne, we had a few problems in the theatre." No shit, I was thinking! "Very rarely, there isn't enough elasticity in the skin to create a suitable pocket for the implant. I realised I had two options, either to stop the procedure, leaving you scarred but with no other change to your breasts, or to do something similar to what we would do with someone who has had reconstructive surgery. Because you were so flat-chested, I had little to work with." I didn't really understand what I was being told. What had he done? The surgeon then explained that he had chosen to continue, but this meant cutting the muscles in my chest and placing the implants between them before sewing the muscles back together. I asked if this was why I was in so much pain and was told it was, and that there were drains around the implants which would have to stay in for the next 24 hours to catch any excess fluid.

I was thinking "What have you done to yourself?!" and that Rachel had been right to tell me to leave my small but healthy breasts alone, I could almost hear her saying "I told you so." My aunt appeared shortly afterwards and tried to cheer me up by asking to look at my new boobs. I couldn't move my arms because I was in so much pain, but indicated that she could lift the blanket. The sight that greeted me was like something out of a freak show. The only way that I can describe what they looked like was like the famous Madonna gold pointed cone bra! My aunt's reaction said it all "Oh dear!" What could I say to that, when this was something that I had inflicted upon myself? There wasn't anything I could say, because "Oh dear!" said it all.

The following day the surgeon came to remove the drains; I was rolled onto my side as each one was pulled out. It wasn't the most comfortable of experiences; I could feel each one unwinding around the implant as it was pulled out. The nurse then put me into a support (like a giant elastic band) which I was to wear for the next three months. The support was worn around my back and under my armpits at the top of my breast implants because apparently the muscles were not strong enough to hold them in place. Should I not wear it I was warned my implants would probably end up too high on my chest. I was also told that I would have to massage my breasts every day to get them into shape, because, again, my body wasn't able to do this on its own.

I went home and did as I was told, even though I have never felt pain like it. For a week I couldn't move my arms even to get myself out of bed. I had to call mum from my mobile phone whenever I needed her to help me. She had to feed me, wash me and assist me with my everyday tasks, including the massage (which hurt like hell). Returning to the clinic ten days later to have my stitches out, I was still concerned at the shape of my boobs and the amount of pain I was still in. I was examined and told not to worry; this was "Exactly what they were meant to look like at this stage." I wasn't entirely convinced, after my last surgery when I had been told the same thing but my concerns had proved to be valid. To appease me, the surgeon told me he would see me every two weeks for the next three months to monitor them for any problems such as capsular contracture or my body rejecting the implants. None of these further complications happened to me, luckily, and after my three month check up I was really very happy with my new breasts. It had been a long and painful road to get here, but I smiled when the Doctor told me they were the best pair he had ever done in 27 years. He even asked to use my pictures in the following year's cosmetic brochure. Looking back now, I guess it was worth the pain, but would I do it again? HELL NO!

Summer, 2000

I had started house sitting for Joy whenever she and her family went away. I loved escaping to their house in the heart of the Peak District and looking after the animals and in particular her horse, Ben. I loved riding him; the power and the control and the simple freedom of being outside was exhilarating. It was such a far cry from where I grew up, and being there made me realise that I wanted much more from my life than I currently had. I had been back at work for just over three months since the operation when I realised that in order to change this life I was living I needed to change myself, I needed some new challenges, I needed anything but to be stuck examining socks and wrapping chips! There was no way I could settle for this existence for the rest of my life - I needed out of the rut that had become my day to day life.

Fortunately, I was bright enough to realise that I needed to take action, rather than just thinking that an alternative life would fall in to my lap. I had so much I wanted to achieve, but nothing had gone to plan. I knew that this was mainly my own fault, but everything seemed out of reach in my current circumstances. My two closest friends, Jennie and Josie, were stay at home mums, which I could appreciate, but which wasn't something that I wanted for myself. I decided that if I started afresh, relocating and finding a new circle of friends (not losing the existing ones of course) maybe I could start again. Perhaps I could even sort myself out too.

June, 2001

I wasn't sure how I was going to achieve this move with no educational qualifications and no experience in anything but menial roles. For months, I sat at the Job Centre every Friday, scrolling through hundreds of jobs on their computers. Eventually, I stumbled across an advert for Group Four Custodial Services, looking for staff to work at Nottingham Crown Court. I had always fancied being in the police or something, and I guess this role was sort of related to that, dealing with prisoners. I had really enjoyed my time with the Army Cadets, and I thought that a police role, or something similar, would give me that same sense of structure, belonging, discipline and control. Maybe because inside I felt so out of control, the idea of being in such a structured environment was appealing. I think on some bizarre level, I also thought that I would be dealing with people who were in some ways even more of a failure, than I was. So, I was intrigued by the ad and decided to apply, following the principle that you have to be in *it to win it*, although I didn't really expect to hear anything.

January, 2002

And I didn't hear anything, for ages. I was really surprised to get a response a few months later explaining that although there were currently no vacancies in Nottingham, Group Four were holding a National Recruitment Day in Milton Keynes. I was invited to attend this 'Training Day' where they would conduct various tests to assess the suitability of applicants.

The Great Escape

My mum was completely shocked when I told her about the job interview in Milton Keynes, and asked me what on earth I would do if it all went wrong. I guess that although I had been (probably too) fiercely independent from a young age, Mum knew from experience that I didn't always make the most sensible decisions. She was probably justified in worrying about me, particularly because in moving away I would be denying her the opportunity to continue to keep an eye on me. I explained to her that I couldn't stay in Huthwaite, living at home and working in a sock factory and a chip shop. I needed something more fulfilling and challenging and I needed to at least try to do this, rather than always wondering what might have been. Mum agreed that she would support me if a 'fresh start and a new life' were really what I wanted.

January 22nd, 2002

I had never been to Milton Keynes before so I decided to travel down the day before both to check the place out and so that I would be refreshed after a good night's sleep in a hotel rather than a long journey down on the morning of the interview. I loved Milton Keynes. I know it gets criticised and that they are prettier places to visit, but it seemed so new and fresh, and so very different from the sleepy small village I'd grown up in. It was the perfect place for my new start. The day itself involved various tests and a formal interview. It was difficult to guess how many people I was competing against, but I was convinced I hadn't done well enough. In particular, one question was: "Let's say you get the job. What would do if you found someone hanging in a vehicle or in a court cell?" After some thought, I answered that as honestly as I could; I had no idea, having never dealt with that kind of situation, but I would hope that I would be equipped to deal with this, and any other scenario, through the appropriate training that I would receive from Group Four. Convinced that I hadn't known or done enough to get the job, I drove back home. Putting the interview to the back of my mind, I was ready to continue with my life as it was, at least for the time being.

I had to have a wisdom tooth removed a couple of days later, and although I was supposed to be working that evening in the chip shop, my dentist had advised me not to. I explained this to my boss, and talked to another girl who had to cover my shift. She wasn't at all happy with the rota change because she had booked to go to see a medium and now she had to work instead. I felt awful, and offered go in her place, so that she wouldn't lose her money. I can't say what I was thinking when I did this, but for some reason that's what happened. I went along with two other women, mother and daughter, from the chip shop. Strange as it may seem, despite my ghostly experience at the factory, my sudden aversion to my bedroom at home, and the dream of my granddad's passing, I really did not believe in mediums and was determined I would expose her as a fraud. I said this to the other two, suggesting that I should go through in the middle of the two of them, so we could see if she spotted the connection between them. They thought this was a great idea.

That evening, at about 6.30pm, we arrived at a little white cottage in a small village nearby. We were greeted by a slim, attractive woman in her early forty's, with long wavy, dark brown hair, who introduced herself as Tasha and then told us she would see "Mum first, followed by daughter with the scar on her stomach, and then you with the tooth last." So much for our plan, but I still wasn't convinced, thinking that maybe the others had let her know that I was coming in the place of the girl who had originally booked this reading, and that they had mentioned my visit to the dentist. I waited for about two hours while the others had their readings, sitting in a wooden rocking chair and reading a book about Tasha's life and how she came to do what she did. Her book contained information about some of the experiences her clients had had, including numerous police forces around the United Kingdom, which she has helped. After the second reading, Tasha walked over to me and almost pinned me in to the chair before snapping "I'm not reading you!" When I asked her why, she replied "Because you don't believe." She was right, I was sceptical, but I simply challenged her to prove me wrong. "I need to clear the other spirits away and speak to my spirit guide first." she said, heading back to her office.

I was still convinced that I would be able to trip Tasha up and prove her to be a fake when she eventually came back into the waiting room.

However, as she approached, she told me that she wouldn't be reading me that night but that she would prove herself to me before I left. She also told me that I would come back to her again sometime in the future (she was right, but it would be over two years later). By now, I was just thinking "Whatever, Lady, just get on with it." Tasha paused, and looked me up and down as if she was assessing me, before she explained "I'm struggling to read you, which has only happened to me a handful of times." She moved closer and we locked eye contact again before she continued "You're blocking me, you have a wall so thickly around you, and I think you have the gift yourself." I laughed at this, which Tasha didn't seem particularly happy about.

A moment or two passed before she spoke to me again, and this time she got my full attention! "I have David here with me and he wants to speak to Susan." I'm not sure if my face gave anything away or whether Tasha could sense the goose bumps rising on my arms, but this time *she* laughed. She laughed loudly and freely, and then paused as if listening to someone talking to her, before she spoke again "David says, don't worry she won't come, she doesn't believe and she won't until they meet again."

As you know, Susan is my mum and David was her brother. David had died from cancer the previous year. Tasha's next comment to me was in the form of a question. "Why should you be called Hannah?" I honestly had no idea what she was talking about here, and I told her as much. Once she had finished what she was saying, I offered her the money for the reading, but Tasha refused to take this from me stating that she just wanted to prove herself to me as being genuine. I left the cottage feeling rather confused, only for Tasha to shout after me "By the way you get the job, you'll find out next week."

As soon as I got home, I told Mum about what had been said, mentioning her brother's name and the job. Ever the sceptic, Mum just laughed at me. When I asked her why my name should be Hannah, however, the colour drained from her face before she told me that this had been the name she would have liked for me.

February 2nd, 2002

I was offered (as predicted by Tasha) the job with Group Four. I was scheduled to start in September, which when I received the letter seemed so far away, but in reality this flew by really quickly, possibly because I was so excited about the new life that lay ahead of me.

September, 2002

My mum and sister were really proud of me and organised a surprise leaving party on the Saturday before I left, with all the family (including my dad and step mum) and my friends. I wasn't supposed to know about it, but one of my friends let it slip. I know she felt terrible, but in all honesty I was grateful, because I hated surprises at the best of times. I promised I would play along and still act surprised. When I got to the party, the only thing I was really surprised and disappointed about was that my dad wasn't there after all. I asked Kelli if he had been invited and she reassured me that of course he had. Mum had called and personally invited him. In fact, she told me, he and his wife had already been to the party. They had arrived earlier, had one drink (without speaking to anyone) and then left before I arrived. Kelli was surprised that I was surprised; she was more conscious of Dad's failings than I was. I felt really let down, and it did put a dampener on my night. I couldn't understand why he wouldn't have been able to wait to see me; I had only been fifteen minutes late. So, I did what I always did: I put on a brave face and went on a mission with the alcohol.

The next day I left for Milton Keynes, where I spent the first six weeks on a training course and in a hotel. I was really lucky because somehow I ended up in a suite with a separate kitchen and lounge, and a four poster bed. There were six of us on the training course staying in the same hotel; we all gelled quickly and it ended up being like a six week party. During that time, I found a house share ready for my proper move to Milton Keynes.

I loaded up my car with all my worldly possessions in black Council bin liners and drove away from the village that I'd spent so many years in, not even looking back once. As I drove away, I turned the radio on to be met by "Here I go again on my own; going down the only road I've ever known!" blasting out. It felt so appropriate, one of those poignant moments which summed up how I felt about my life: me, myself, on my own as always.

I had chosen to house share because I thought it would be a great way to meet new friends having moved to a new town. The house itself wasn't what I would have chosen to live in, but it was OK. I shared with three other girls, two of whom were great fun and easy to get along with, the other was OK, but a bit quiet. Although it was great, I missed home much more than I had expected to and most weekends when I wasn't working I would drive back to visit. After a few months, I forced myself to stop doing this. I had to face up to being somewhere new and to making a new life here or what was the point? I decided to only go home every three or four months, which was really hard at first because this was the first time I'd lived away from home. It was great fun too, though, because I no longer had to answer to anyone. My partying got worse and worse. I continued to mask my insecurities and to hide the burden of Annie by drowning them out with alcohol. When I was drunk, I was the fun and lively party girl, full of confidence. Everyone wanted to be my friend. So in summary, I had relocated to start again and to try to make something of my life, but here I was continuing on my path of self-destruction. And now it was even easier, as there was no one to supervise me!

December, 2002

I had been living in Milton Keynes for about three months and was really enjoying my new job. I would be part of a crew taking people to and from court and prison. As the new girl on the block, I was 'polyfilla', fitting in as an when required rather than working with a set 'crew partner' as those who had been there longer tended to do. One morning, I was greeted at the control room by a guy in his fifties who I hadn't worked with before "Morning, Poppet, you're stuck with me this week!" he exclaimed. I extended my hand to shake his, and Davie took me by surprise, turning my hand over and kissing the back of it, like a real old-school gentleman would. As Davie ran through the vehicle checks before we left, one of the girls in the office commented that I'd got a "Good one there." She went on to explain that everyone wanted to be Davie's partner, but that his permanent buddy was Jean. She reckoned there was a waiting list, but the only fair thing would be to put everyone's name in a hat when Jean retired.

As the week went on, Davie and I really clicked and had such a laugh with each other. On the Friday we were sent on a run to Great Yarmouth Magistrates Court. We did our drop and were empty of prisoners, so I was now in the front of the cab for our drive back to the base in Milton Keynes. I nudged Davie, "You know what?" I asked, "No, what?" "I have a random urge to build a sandcastle!" Davie just looked at me and burst out laughing. "Are you serious?" I think he thought I was joking! "Yup, deadly!" I reached in to my bag, got out my purse, and asked Davie to stop at a sea-front shop. Of course, because it was December and out of season, none of the sea front shops were open; but I wasn't going to let that stop *me*! I climbed into the back of the van and retrieved some polystyrene cups. I jumped back out like a crazy child on a mission and ran to the beach where I built (in the pouring rain!) the first sandcastle I had made since the age of about seven. Davie just sat in the cab laughing at me.

I got back in the cab soaked and cold and Davie handed me a towel, saying "You're bonkers, girl!" I chuckled and responded "Life is for living, and you should treat every day as your last!" It's ironic given the mental, emotional and physical issues I was dealing with inside, but my bubbly persona ensured that Annie and my other problems were safely tucked away in secret, were no one could see them. On the drive back to base, Davie asked me to crew up with him permanently. I wasn't too sure about this at first, because he had worked with Jean for several years and I didn't want to step on anyone's toes. However, by the end of the trip we both agreed that this is what we wanted to do.

Arriving back at the base, Davie jumped out of the cab and ran around the front of the van to open my door. I jumped out of the cab and grabbed his hand, and we skipped in to the Control Room like a pair of giggling children. Davie walked up to the crew board and moved Jean's name, putting mine in its place. Then with a red marker he wrote 'we want to be together', before grabbing my hand and skipping back out. Not a word was said. The faces of the controllers were a picture!

I wasn't sure what to expect going back to work the next week. I felt really bad for Jean, but knew my job would be much more fun from now on if I was working with Davie. I wasn't sure if I would be with Davie anyway, as we had only, in effect, made a *request*, and we hadn't done that in the most conventional way! Thankfully, I had absolutely nothing to worry about. It seemed that Jean had wanted to reduce her hours, work part time and move to the immigration side of things anyway, but she had been scared of upsetting Davie by telling him this, so it was win-win all round.

Around this time, I began to keep a diary as a way for me to vent my feelings. In some ways, I hoped that by putting them down on paper it would help, as it would feel as if the feelings had gone away once I put my pen down and closed the diary, but of course they hadn't.

Diary entry: December 12th, 2002: I HATE FOOD, I HATE FOOD, I HATE FOOD AND THE FACT IT CONTROLS ME!!!! I CAN'T STAND TO FEEL IT INSIDE ME FOR MORE THAN TEN MINUTES! It repulses me down to my core, but at least I don't have to hide like I did at home, I can do it much more easily . . .

As Christmas approached, Davie and I got into the festive spirit and decorated our van, including a Christmas tree with flashing lights and a singing Rudolf that sat in the back to keep me company. We were made to take them down in January; otherwise I think they would have stayed up all year round. As the weeks went on Davie and I got to know one another really well. Spending up to twelve hours a day with someone, you have to get along! He soon realised that my persona was just a front and that the loud and bubbly Joanne was fake. Although he never knew the pain and anguish I was hiding, he saw a quieter, more considerate side to me, and described me as "A big softy, who would do anything for anyone."

Diary entry: January 8th, 2003: I think every time I feel I need to eat I should take a trip to the mirror, just to remind myself how fat and ugly I really am! Look at me. Seriously, I am fucking disgusting, even surgery has not helped make me thin and beautiful enough to be in this world! The makeup is my mask that I can hide behind to pretend everything is OK. I keep smiling while inside I'm dying.

As my dissatisfaction and poor body image still hadn't been appeased by the results of my surgery, I had now turned to makeup in order to try, once more, to make myself beautiful. I wouldn't go anywhere, and I mean *anywhere*, without my full makeup on. So now Joanne had a literal mask as well as my personality mask!

February 14th, 2003

On Valentine's Day, I climbed into the back of the van to find that Davie had bought me a bunch of flowers (from his dog Kiri!). The card simply said, "Because beautiful women should always get flowers today." He could be so sweet, but he was also a terror and we totally bounced off of each other and wound each other up something chronic! At one stage, I had the opportunity of a free holiday to Lanzarote, but I only had three days notice before the flight. Davie told me to throw a sickie, as I would never get the time off. I just couldn't bring myself to do it, and instead put in a request for leave, which was of course refused, as we had both expected. The day that I was supposed to fly, I got into work as usual to find that Davie was there early, with a naughty grin on his face. "What's up with you?" I asked. I was soon to find out. As I was climbing the steps to get into the back of the van, all I could hear from behind me was Davie laughing. I poked my head around the van door, not knowing what to expect. The entire area was covered in pictures of Lanzarote! Davie had been to the travel agents to get brochures and had ripped out all the pages and stuck them around van! I glared at him, but I could never be angry with him for long, because he would always put on those puppy-dog eyes! Soon I was laughing, as he explained "Well, Poppet, if you can't go to Lanzarote, I'll bring Lanzarote to you!"

Easter Bank Holiday Monday 2003

I was working at St Albans Magistrates Court, when an outside call came through on my mobile phone. Normally my phone would have been off or on silent, but I must have forgotten. I saw that it was Jennie's mum's home number, which I thought was strange, because it wasn't often she called me, so I decided I should answer the call. In fact, it was Jennie's dad on the line. "Joanne. I have some bad news." I just listened and couldn't say anything "Joanne, its Jennie. She's dead – she killed herself." I slid down the wall of the office, feeling hot and faint. Finally, I managed to speak "Are you joking?" I couldn't believe that's what I had said, but that was what came out. I didn't cry, I couldn't speak, I just sat on the office floor holding the phone to my ear. Someone must have gone to get Davie from court, because the next thing I knew, he was picking me up off the floor and carrying me out to the van. He put me in the cab before holding my hands and speaking to me like a dad would. "Poppet, what's wrong? What's happened?" He could obviously tell that it was something really bad. All I could say was "I need a cigarette. Please, get me a cigarette." Davie hated me smoking and was always on at me to quit, but this day he actually lit the cigarette for me.

Davie held my hand, saying nothing as I sat smoking in silence. I finally told him what had happened, but I still couldn't cry. I was seething with anger at Jennie; I couldn't believe that she had done this. I couldn't believe she had left her two beautiful daughters. How could she do this to her family, how could she do this to me? How dare she! Sure we had grown apart a little, particularly since I'd moved away, but I was still her best friend. Why hadn't she talked to me? I would have always been there for her, no matter what, day and night. All she had to do was pick up the phone and I would have been there in a flash. Surely she knew this.

Jennie's funeral was obviously very tough and emotional, but I still wasn't really acknowledging how I felt. Back at work, Davie was the person who let me off-load and vent about my anger towards her, but in reality, to a large degree, I was blocking my mixed emotions like I always did with everything. I pushed them to one side, because if I didn't have to face the problem and deal with it, the problem didn't exist, right?

Wrong! In reality I once again turned to other things, and to Alcohol and Annie, to help me cope and numb the pain I was feeling. I was binging over ten times a day again. Things had got so bad that I no longer needed to put my fingers down my throat, I could purge with no assistance. I also discovered laxatives as an additional purge method. What I didn't realise though, was just how worried people were becoming about me. Obviously my mask had been slipping a little. This only came to light when I passed out in Ribbleton Prison's reception one morning. As always, though, my quick thinking kicked in, and I took a few days off, pretending to be ill. I was drowning my sorrows even more than usual. I was drinking so much that at times I was in work when I really shouldn't have been, because I wasn't fit. I was often badly hung-over or still felt drunk. On one occasion I was so ill I even threw up in a prison property bag. As we approached Goadhurst Prison, I disposed of the bag in the bin just outside the gatehouse.

Diary Entry: August 14th, 2003: SKINNY=BEAUTIFUL I am FAT and UGLY! FAT and UGLY! FAT and UGLY! FAT and UGLY. That is all I will ever be good at being! I'm so fat, it's beyond disgusting! I'm so scared to trust anyone, because anyone who promised to be there for me, well, they always left! I just realised I'll never see my best friend again...

Gradually, I started to relax a little, and Davie and I began have some fun trips again. On day, we picked up at Milton Keynes police station and off we set for the Isle of Wight Magistrates Court. On the journey to the ferry port, I warned Davie that I suffered really badly from sea sickness, "Poppet, you can't possibly get sea sick on a ferry to the Isle of Wight, it's like crossing a big pond!" he exclaimed, laughing when I assured him that I could get sea sick on a lilo in a swimming pool.

Once we'd driven onto the ferry, Davie came round to the back of the van to see how I was. He stood in the door way, bouncing on the steps, I think he thought I had been winding him up, about getting sea sick; he soon found out the hard way that I wasn't! We dropped off at the court and took a lunch break, walking around town. We decided to post something back to base, and packaged up a postcard (with hugs and kisses from the Isle of Wight) in a property bag containing a sample of sand and a plastic crab! This was the first of many random items to be sent back to base from our adventures!

I think, the whole time that we worked together, Davie and I only had one disagreement, which was when he was tormenting me for leaving our paperwork behind at court, adding two hours to our day. I can honestly say Group Four has to be the best job I have ever had thanks to Daddy Davie.

The Fab Four

Davie was a great male role model, and continues to be a dear friend. Unfortunately, my personal relationships with other men during my ten years in Milton Keynes haven't been as successful. I decided to write about my relationships in one separate chapter, rather than within the main body of the book, so that I could protect the innocent, as well as the friends and family of the maybe not so innocent.

Describing my relationships here means that only those close to me, and the men themselves, will know who they are; but including them does provide a fuller picture of what Joanne was going through.

During my ten years in Milton Keynes, I have been emotionally involved with four men. I will refer to them simply as John, Paul, George and Ringo for the purpose of this book. I haven't put everything in the right order, for the sake of discretion.

I have tended to look up to the men in my life, to put them on a pedestal and often be treated like shit in return. I would never fight back, having always had the 'discuss and move on' approach to disagreements. I've never had the self-confidence to scream and shout or get physical anyway. I'm a tactile person, with very old fashioned values. I enjoy looking after people, because I am a natural care bear at heart, and a hopeless romantic. Having said that, I have caused hurt as well as been the victim of it. Hey, I was emotionally screwed up, what do you expect?!

108

Anyway, my relationships . . . let's start with **John**. Here, I was the victim of a mentally abusive relationship that almost tipped me over the edge on more than one occasion. I couldn't do anything right by John, no matter how hard I tried. I was so downtrodden and insecure that I felt I didn't deserve anything better and I didn't have the energy to fight back. I looked up to John for a long time, and treated him like a God.

Don't get me wrong, when this relationship was good, it was amazing! But when it was bad it was beyond awful. I know John loved me, he really did love me; but I wonder whether he actually loved me too much, almost to the point of obsession, which in itself was not healthy.

I am not saying I was an angel in this relationship, because I was far from it. In fact, I made a terrible mistake right at the beginning of our time together. I had had five or six dates with John when someone who I had known for many years made a pass at me. It was a only brief kiss and I pushed him away. I decided to be honest about this and tell John the truth because I didn't want 'us', to start out on a lie! BIG MISTAKE! Maybe, after he picked up his glass walked in to the garden and threw it against the wall, I should have seen what was coming and walked away from the relationship there and then, but I didn't. After this insight into John's anger, I just used to tell him what I thought he wanted to hear and I lied about the extent of my problems with food. I used to trust John completely, and let him know all the passwords for my online accounts etc, but then I found out he had been checking up on me and looking at the sites I had been visiting.

He had caught me out. I had been looking at pro-anorexia sites having told him that I wasn't and I wouldn't, but of course he had breached my trust too, by spying on me. John wouldn't believe me when I told him these sites actually helped me to reduce the binging. These women understood what I was going through and we could talk openly and honestly, with none of the judgemental looks or comments that I sometimes received from him or my friends, who could never truly understand me like these other women did.

It's very difficult, when you're having the think about how to behave and to keep someone happy, to always get it right. Once, John and I were out with my friend Emma and her partner, playing pool. John had been showing off and wasn't being very pleasant. To avoid making a scene, I walked away, pretending to go to the bathroom. Later that evening, we had the argument that I'd been trying to avoid anyway, because apparently *I* had embarrassed *him* by walking away. In the early hours of the morning, he stormed off, away from me and my friends, and walked sixteen miles home!

On another occasion, John attacked a friend of mine, who I had just met for a coffee after a night out. There were four of us, we had shared a taxi home, but John was convinced there was more to my friendship with this particular person, and so he ran past me, knocking me off my feet before punching him. He even smashed his windows, which I ended up paying for. John could find a reason to argue and fight over anything. If I tried to treat him to something, it usually backfired. Instead of being pleased and grateful and appreciating my good intentions, John would tell me exactly what I had got wrong. It was *always* my fault.

For Christmas one year, I brought him a car and driving lessons because he couldn't drive; I had spent weeks trying to organise this surprise with his dad; but this was thrown back in my face after yet another disagreement; which again was twisted to end up as my fault.

John once told me that I had to choose between him and my mum, when she heard the way he spoke to me and told him never to speak to me like that again. His own mum had also told him numerous times that he shouldn't speak to me the way he did. Still, the rocky relationship continued, and somehow we ended up engaged and even planning for a wedding. And then John gambled away our wedding savings!

Why I didn't get out much sooner? I wanted to, but I didn't know how to. Towards the end, I cared more about John's family than about him, and I didn't want to lose them because they treated me like their daughter and had allowed me into that stereotypical family unit which I had always craved. Some time after we split up, John convinced me he had changed. We got back together for a short while and it was really good, but the first time we had a disagreement, he threw my eating disorder in my face. By this time, however, I was a much stronger person and ended it right there and then. Moral of the story? Never go back.

Paul was a terrible accident, a stupid, terrible accident that if I could turn back the clock and erase, then I really would! Paul was a married man that I ended up having an affair with. He is one of my biggest regrets in life. This all happened after a very boozy night, so boozy that I didn't even know a thing about it until the morning after; until I was stirring and heard someone snoring at the side of me. It was a real SNAFU moment (military sarcasm: Situation Normal: All Fucked Up), as I opened one eye, looked to the right of me and thought 'OH FUCK. I lifted the duvet to confirm my worst fears. I was naked. I must have done. If only I could remember! This one-off indiscretion was bad enough, but somehow I found myself agreeing that as long as no one EVER found out and as long as neither of us got emotionally involved, then it was what it was: sex. I had not long since been hurt for the first time, and I figured that this relationship would be safe. I wouldn't get emotionally involved, so I couldn't be hurt again. I was desperate to be desired. I needed to be wanted. I longed to feel something, because anything was better than feeling nothing. I justified this by allowing myself to believe that I was doing nothing wrong, because *I* wasn't cheating on anyone. But I knew he was married so yes, I was in the wrong.

This relationship carried on for about a year within very strict rules. I never contacted Paul. Neither of us told anyone and he never questioned me dating anyone else, because technically I was single. This arrangement worked out well for us both and we each got what we wanted from it, until one night when the rules got broken.

We were out dancing when Paul said "Joanne, I am really falling for you. I can't stop thinking about you." I laughed this off and put it down to the fact he had been drinking. When he called me later that week, I pretended I was going out already and couldn't see him (In fact, I was in my pyjamas, reading a book). When Paul questioned who I was going out with, I knew he had meant what he said, and for me that was it, he had broken the rules and I now had to deal with the mess that I had helped to create. I was still wondering how I was going to handle the situation ten minutes later, when Paul turned up on my doorstop telling me he wanted to leave his wife. I laughed at him and slammed the door in his face. I haven't spoken to him since. Believe me, I know how bad that sounds, but Joanne wasn't the person I am today; I would NEVER do these things now. I was a very damaged young woman back then. (Not that this excuses my past behaviour).

George was a player, and I guess you could call him Karma's revenge for my affair with Paul. He pounced on me when I was at my most vulnerable and I fell for his smooth talk, really believing he was different. George picked me up when he had nothing better to do and put me down again when he got bored, but George I cared about a great deal. George I was a total fool with; I was a big, hopeless, romantic with

MYSELF, ME AND I

George and I would have done (and did do) anything for him, even when he let me down time and time again, by cancelling our plans or simply not bothering to turn up at all.

When I surprised him with a romantic trip to Paris for his birthday (including an opportunity to see his favourite band), George was listening to them with me while he was texting someone else! But, as always, I forgave him. Stupidly, I thought I could change him and make him love me. I finally realised that the only person George loved was George, when I was rushed in to hospital. I had spent the night before with him, and he had told me that he loved me and that he wanted us to have a future together, as of now. It would be a fresh start and I should get a toothbrush to leave at his; he would clear some space in the closet for me to leave some clothes too. I was so happy at this thought. When the nurse asked who I wanted to be informed where I was, I asked for her to call George for me. He didn't even bother to answer his phone. The nurse left a voicemail, with all the information, saying to contact me as soon as he got the message. He did so, *by text*! He explained that couldn't come and get me because he was 'busy'! It wasn't even the fact he couldn't drop whatever it was he was doing to be there for me, at my side. What was worse was that I wasn't even worth a phone call to see whether I was OK or not. I would have dropped everything to support George had our situations been reversed. I really do pick them, don't I?!

Last but not least we have **Ringo**, who appeared in my life in the wrong place and at the wrong time.

114

Ringo I did fall in love with and, if I'm totally honest, I still love him today. Typical, hey? I didn't ever tell him. I couldn't tell him. Because I needed to sort myself out and get to where I am now in life, before letting anyone else in to my heart. There is nothing more I can say about that. I was once told "If you love someone, set them free; if they come back then it's meant to be."

After these relationships, I then took two years out to learn about myself and to get myself well. I became what I call to some of my friends a non-practicing lesbian! It's great, and I would recommend that all women do this at some point in their lives. Why? Because to be loved, REALLY loved, you need to love, respect and accept yourself. Once you believe this, you'll realise that you are already a fulfilled person; stable, functional, and happy, with a career, friends and hobbies. You don't need another person to make you whole. I would now rather spend the rest of my life single and happy, than miserable and in the wrong relationship. But, I'm getting way ahead of myself. My journey continues in the next chapter, and I have a long way to go before I get anywhere close to feeling this positive about myself.

Diary entry: January 6th, 2004: I am not going to make my goal of 24 hours, but 23 is close enough! Just one more hour DON'T EAT FOOD, DON'T EAT FOOD, DON'T EAT FOOD, DON'T EAT FOOD, DON'T EAT FOOD, DON'T EAT FOOD, DON'T EAT FOOD, DON'T EAT FOOD!

The Big Brother House

April 14th, 2004

I was twenty five when I moved on from Group Four to join the Prison Service. I had been used to working with prisoners, and this seemed a logical progression into a job where there would be more career development opportunities. But how on earth did someone with so many issues manage to take on such a role? My acting skills had been honed to an Oscar-winning level, that's how! I also still believed that here I would find people more screwed up than I was. In this environment, it would be easier for me to look normal. Also, although Group Four had been great, it was a difficult routine in terms of your personal and social life because you could never plan anything; there was always the likelihood that you would end up on the other side of the country having to cancel yet another event. I was looking forward to a more structured working routine.

During my Prison Service training, I shadowed a Prison Officer called Emma who was working on House Unit Three at Ribbleton Prison; she was to be one of my mentors during my probationary period. I wasn't too sure what to make of Emma at first, but after I jumped in and became involved in a situation that I wasn't supposed to (until fully trained), we seemed to click, and from then on got on like a house on fire. I had been with Emma and the Wing Senior Officer when they had to restrain a prisoner. I'd looked around for some assistance, because restraint is something that should always be done in

116

threes, but there was no one else nearby. So, with my Group Four training behind me, I hit the nearest alarm and then jumped on the prisoner's remaining free arm. Not the usual way of breaking the ice with someone, but it worked for me and Emma! Other people were surprised that we got on so well because we were both rather loud and they assumed our personalities would clash, but the opposite seemed to be true.

While at Group Four, I had been sharing a house with a girl who ran a beauty business from home, which meant I could never really relax and slob about in my pyjamas in case a client arrived; because of this, it never truly felt like home. I decided that with the move to the Prison Service I would look for somewhere new to live. On the training course I met Brett, who needed somewhere to live because he was moving to Milton Keynes from Birmingham. We decided we would rent something together if we could find anything suitable. We managed to find a three bedroom house in Emerson Valley, and one of my girlfriends from a previous house share moved in with us.

After just eight weeks of Prison Service training we had our Passing-Out Parade, where we would all be presented with certificates by a local councillor. Families were invited, and I really wanted both Mum and Dad to be there. I called Mum first and asked her if she was OK with me inviting Dad and his wife Jan along too. Of course, as always, she was very supportive and told me it was *my* day and I could invite whoever I wanted to. On the day itself, I was a nervous wreck; my Training Senior Officer even asked me if I was OK, because he'd never seen me looking so worried. I had the biggest knot in my stomach; my parents hadn't been in the same room together for so many years and I knew they couldn't stand each other. I wondered what on earth I'd let myself in for; how would they cope at such close proximity? Thankfully, I needn't have worried and they each behaved very well, even agreeing to me having a photo taken with both of them together. It was just after this that Dad let me down again. I had wanted everyone to come back to my house for a drink and something to eat; Dad and Jan made their excuses and rushed off at the first opportunity. Still, at least he had made the effort for once to be there for me, I guess that's something right!

Diary Entry: June 3rd, 2004: To get up and purge or not get up and purge? ALWAYS purge, because I'm weak. I think I'm just going to eat Granny Smiths from now on. They're only sixty calories. Then I wouldn't have to purge anymore.

The following week, I started work on House Unit Three. This turned out to be a great place for me to start my prison career because the people I was working with had similar personalities and we all loved a good time on the lash! Although, of course, in reality I was simply hiding my emotional pain at the bottom of the glass. The fact that everyone else loved going out just made this easier for me to do. There were six House Units at Ribbleton, and we named the local pub, the Nut & Squirrel, House Unit Seven. We would head there most lunchtimes, and meet there again after work, after a quick visit home just to get changed. Soon, we were regularly having parties back at my house share too, which then became known as the Big Brother House. We partied as if it was going out of fashion; for the year that I was there you never knew quite who you would find sleeping on the lounge floor when you woke up!

Before one of my many house parties, Emma asked if she could bring along her lodger Becky, who also worked at the prison. Naturally I assured her that my attitude was the more the merrier, although I didn't know Becky well. After an hour or so, Emma asked me what I thought of Becky. When I explained that I had not really had time to form an opinion, she told me that Becky was convinced that I did not like her. I immediately went over and confronted Becky (nicely!) asking why she thought I didn't like her. She laughed nervously and played with her hair as she explained that apparently I never spoke to her at work and I'd blanked her a few times when I worked on her unit. I laughed and apologised, saying that it certainly hadn't been intentional; I was probably just preoccupied as always. A few weeks later, Becky rented the house opposite mine and we soon became good friends.

Diary entry: August 29th, 2004: Right, I have until October to lose 17kg. What is the motivation for this and can I download it? If you want to be pretty you won't eat until you reach this, because eating only makes you fat! Yeah, the whole eating thing didn't work out and now I feel like a whale. I couldn't even discipline myself for one fucking day . . .

So, another diary entry, and another reminder of what was *really* going on for me, for Joanne. But at the same time, my escapism into drink provided huge entertainment for others, as well as reinforcing my emotional mask. Alcohol allowed me to step into the shoes of the carefree and bubbly person I longed to be, and boy did I fill those shoes in style!

While writing this book, I asked some friends from this time to remind me of some of my drunken antics. They didn't disappoint, and had lots of stories they could remind me of. One friend even emailed me and asked "How much room do you have in your inbox?" My current lodger Erica helped me to sift the responses, and having read about everything that Joanne had got up to asked "Who is this person, and why have I never met her?" Of course, now that I am Jo, now that I am I, I don't need to go to these extremes and I'm happy to chill with good food, music, candles and maybe just a couple of glasses of red wine (Gosh, I sound old and boring!). In any case, here are some of my escapades from roughly between the ages of twenty and thirty. Its funny isn't it, the English language? *Escapades*. Maybe I wasn't the first person to use such behaviour as a means of escape from reality.

So, according to my friends, Joanne . . .

- . . . Once instigated a piggy back race through the ski dome in Milton Keynes;
- . . . I have ridden the famous concrete cows of Milton Keynes like a cowgirl – shouting Ye-ha;
- . . . I have had a space hopper race down the street, at 1am and wearing 5 inch heels!

(How I didn't break my ankle I will never know);

- . . . I once protested the fact that no one would go out clubbing with me by holding a one woman sit-down protest in the middle of the street. (Unfortunately, I was surrounded by friends who were also prison colleagues and so I was simply relocated to the house using fully approved control and restraint techniques);

- . . . I borrowed a blow up doll (don't ask!) and made it argue with a cab driver until he finally agreed to take me home from an Hawaiian evening: "Mr Taxi driver, you would be quicker taking me and my friend home than trying to evict us from the back of your cab!";

- . . . I rode on an elephant's head, down Walking Street in Thailand;

- . . . I have climbed a snow 'mountain' in the USA (a *huge* pile of snow cleared into the corner of a car park) while demanding 'Dip Dip' from Chick-fil-A (the equivalent of shouting for ketchup from KFC!). (I'm told video evidence exists of this, and of the snow angel I subsequently did in the middle of the snow mountain!);

- . . . I approached the milk man in my undies at 4.45am, asking for a pint of full fat milk (this was a dare!); and finally;

- . . . I have silenced an entire karaoke bar in Belgium by singing (far too loud) "That's why I'm EASY, easy like Sunday morning."

Anyway, that gives you a flavour of my party-girl persona, the Joanne that everyone saw, the Joanne that was desperate to be liked and desperate to please and yet managed to hide her inner turmoil so well.

2004 was the year that I went back to see Tasha. I guess I was looking for answers, after my first visit to her and having since lost Jennie. I asked Jennie's mum, Elizabeth, if she wanted to come with me, but she said it was too soon for her. She made me promise to pass on anything I heard. Without that commitment I think I would have kept the details of the evening to myself, rather than risk upsetting Elizabeth further, but now I had promised . . .

As I arrived back at Tasha's little white cottage, again I wasn't sure what to expect. I went into a modest room for my reading and sat opposite Tasha at a small table with a CD recorder on it, which she explained would provide a recording of our conversation. There was no other furniture. The room, and Tasha herself, were calm and still, and I didn't feel scared or uncomfortable, although I was aware that while she spoke to me I kept looking over my right shoulder, where I could see what I would describe dust particles shining like tiny fire flies against the wall. I also had a strange sensation similar to when you feel as if you're being watched. Tasha must have noticed my glances, and finally asked "What can you see? Can you see your grandma?" I laughed and said of course not. "Then why do you keep looking over your shoulder?" she asked.

When I told her I didn't know, she placed her hand over mine, on the table, and replied "You know you can see her if you want to. I know you've seen a spirit before, so why do you block it?" "Block what?" I asked her. "Your gift." I snatched my hand away from her, because now she *was* beginning to freak me out. I am not sure if I wanted to get up and run as fast as I ever had at this point or if I was frozen stiff with fear, but what happened next left me completely speechless. Tasha put her finger to her lips as if to say 'shhhhhh'. I did as I was told and just sat watching her. She turned to the recorder and said "This is a message for Elizabeth. I need to see you. Jennie wants to talk to you." Now I know that you may find this hard to believe, and I know how totally insane it sounds, but this happened right in front of me. I don't think *I* would have believed it either if had I not witnessed it with my own eyes.

Tasha then turned back to me and told me things that no one could know about me. She knew I was ill, and kept rubbing her stomach and stroking her neck and asking why did I do it? I was also told that in order to get well I needed to move. Tasha then asked me to join her Development Circle so I could explore 'my gift' further! Needless to say, I declined, but my mind was completely blown by the events of the evening. I went round to see Elizabeth (Tilly, as she is known to friends and family) straight after my reading. As I walked into the house, she asked me if I had heard anything from Jennie, and I told her to listen to the CD. I wouldn't have felt at all comfortable telling her something without any evidence, but the CD spoke for itself. I would love to find that CD now and listen to it again. I also wish I could rationalise the things that Tasha told me about myself; I know you couldn't find that much information on me even now, if you did an internet search on me.

I returned to Milton Keynes a few days later, thinking about what I had been told. I felt as if, for the first time ever, I really wanted to be well, I wanted to sort myself out. Deep, deep down somewhere inside me I wanted to do it, but it would still take me another five years to actually achieve it.

December 25th, 2004

This was to be my first Christmas Day where I would be working, alongside Emma, Tim (one of our partying group), and my lodger Brett. A couple of weeks before, I asked what their plans were and found that none of them had set arrangements, so I asked if they all would like to have Christmas dinner with me after work. Everyone jumped at this idea. I busied myself in the run up to the event, getting organised and buying them all table gifts. I wanted this to be a day to really remember; it was my first Christmas away from my family and I was to play host! We all worked on the same unit and during the shift I discovered that another colleague (who we didn't socialise with) was also alone with no one to spend the day with. Emma knew exactly what I was thinking as I found this out, and said "Joanne, please don't." But there was no way I could let anyone spend Christmas Day on their own. A few weeks earlier, I had thought that that was what I was destined to do, and it hadn't been a nice feeling. I walked over to B Wing to invite him along for the evening.

Steven was resistant at first, saying that he didn't really know me, but I told him he'd get to know me if he came long, and so, having finally convinced him, I scribbled my address down, popped it into his top pocket and told him "7pm sharp, or it's going in the dog!" Before heading back to A wing.

It was a great evening. I was pleased that Steven did join us, although I think he had been a bit shocked to be asked. I even managed to find a large bar of chocolate (hidden in the cupboard) to wrap up for him as his table gift so he didn't feel left out. As the night went on Steven left, so just the four of us remained. The drinks were flowing nicely, and I'd put on some very relaxing music so we were enjoying the quiet post-work and post-meal lull. I was beginning to feel a little tipsy and had the sudden urge to liven up the party. I ran up stairs, grabbed my king size duvet, and sat on it to slide back down the stairs, shouting "Choo, Choo!" Emma, Tim and Brett were sat in fits of laughter, but I convinced them to join me and this is how we spent the last ten minutes of Christmas 2004, so childish but such a giggle.

February 2005

My weight had been yo-yoing from anywhere in between 8 stone 7lb and 11 stone! It's easy to spot an anorexic, but people aren't as attuned, and it's not as obvious when someone is bulimic, so no one seemed to guess. Annie had been more in my life than she hadn't recently, and in fact had become a Grand Master at our game of hide and seek.

Diary Entry: February 3rd, 2005: think positive and positive things will happen! Why can't you just be happy with yourself? Because I'm fat and ugly, that's why. I can be standing in a crowd of a thousand people but no one knows what goes on inside my head. The only real conversation I have is with Annie because I am alone even in a room full of people no one really knows me! Think positive? Ha ha, just no.

Diary Entry: March 23rd, 2005: just looking in the mirror brings me close to tears, I may be still young, but my life is already so screwed up! Just look up the words fat, ugly and failure! FAT – you will see my ass, UGLY – you will see my face, and FAILURE – you will see a picture of me eating.

April, 2005

I had decided that I wanted to buy a property and settle more permanently in Milton Keynes, now I had finally found a flat that I liked and moved out of the Big Brother House. Moving in to my own property was great; it was mine to do with as I pleased. I decorated it and bought everything I wanted to make it my own little sanctuary, where I could escape from the world. I also managed to take up some healthier activities once I left the Big Brother House. I no longer went out every night, I started horse riding again and I was walking fairly regularly too. I loved nothing more than escaping over to the Cotswolds, Mendips or Malvern's when I had some time off work, which wasn't often. I worked so many hours overtime and also took in a lodger, not because I needed the money, but because I had set myself the target of being mortgage free by the time I was 35, which gave me nine years.

January, 2006

I opted for Liposuction round three (Sorry Mum, I think I forgot to mention this!). I had spoken to Emma, who was concerned about this and asked why I simply couldn't accept myself for who I was. I promised her that I would "Once this was done." A few days later I was called in for my quarterly review at work. I was absolutely horrified when my manager said "Here Jo, I hear that you're going to have a little nip and tuck?" How on earth did he know that?! "There isn't much that Ra-de, Ra-de doesn't know in this place!" he told me. He then asked me why. I looked at him and replied in a sarcastic tone "Because I have a big fat ass!" Tony smiled and declared that there was nothing wrong with me, before he said that he could save me three grand and my arse would look fantastic! "Dare I ask how?" He laughed, and then in typical prison officer black humour continued, "Put your cheeks on my cheeks and your ass would look great from where I am sitting!" If this had been anyone else I think I would have been offended, but I knew Tony too well. I burst out laughing before slapping him and telling him that after a comment like that I expected to get an exceeded on my annual appraisal!

February, 2006

This time, I attended a clinic in London for my Liposuction. On this occasion, everything went well and I had no complications, *and* the results were obvious and happened quickly! Did this help? Was I happy with my new shape and size? Come on, you know me well enough by now! I've let you see behind the mask, behind the party animal, to the scared and unhappy girl hiding away. Of course the answer is no.

Joanne was still there for all to see, but Annie visited so very often that it was so tiring, so exhausting, a cycle of binging and purging that I just couldn't escape. My bulimia was getting worse and worse that even my dentist made reference to it, because the enamel on my teeth was being affected and my gums had started to recede, due to the contact with my stomach acid each time I purged. I tried to deny the situation, saying he must be mistaken, but he cautioned me that he had seen the same symptoms many times over the years. He wasn't telling me what to do, but he did want to prevent me from causing any more damage to my teeth than I had already caused. He asked if I cleaned my teeth straight after purging and I replied indignantly that of course I did. The dentist told me I needed to stop doing that and to make sure I didn't have any acidic drinks for at least three hours after purging. He went on to explain that I should just rinse my mouth with warm water, and if I really needed to brush, for hygiene, then I should invest in a soft baby's toothbrush (and still only use warm water to brush with). This would limit further damage to my teeth and gums. He also recommended that from now on I visit him every three months instead of six. Finally, he said, after I struggled to lift my eyes to look at him. "The best thing you can do, Joanne, is to get some professional help."

March, 2006

I really wanted to stop, but I couldn't. Every time I ate something, within a matter of minutes I felt sick. My body was so used to this pattern that I could no longer control it! I tried to resist time and time again and would sit heaving on the sofa or busy myself with inane tasks to try distract my mind, until I couldn't take it no more and rushed into the bathroom. The satisfaction and relief that I would feel following my purges were feelings that I can only describe as the best high, or the most amazing rush in the world, once I had finished with the purges I would instantaneously have control of myself again.

One evening I was over at Emma's house having dinner. We'd had a lovely time, but I was painfully aware that I had to leave within thirty minutes of eating so that I could throw up in private. I had cut it close and I knew that I had to make a move. Emma then questioned me "Joanne, why do you always rush off so soon?" Out came the usual lies. I told her it was getting late and I had an early start in the morning. I felt so bad not being honest with Emma, but I was on the verge of throwing up on her living room floor. "I'm on early too," Emma replied, "You may as well stay over and then we can have a glass of wine." I was so close to getting caught out!

Quickly, I picked up my bag and headed for the door, explaining weakly that I didn't have my uniform with me; if only she'd asked me earlier I would have come prepared. I got in the car aware with every fibre of my body that that had been far too close for comfort. I knew I would never get home in time and pulled my car into a lay-by on the A5 to do something I hadn't done since I had left home; I found a tree to purge behind.

As I got into bed that evening, I prayed for someone or something to give me the strength to take control and stop this. Annie had become so strong that I could almost hear her talking to me as if she was a real person.

March 16th, 2006

I woke up as normal and looked in the mirror, I was looking particularly scrawny of late, which pleased me no end, but what did the scales say? "First," said Annie, "You need to take yourself to the bathroom and do two things. Purge and wee. Purge, regardless of the fact that you haven't eaten since your last purge – you did have a drink, remember. And wee. Just sit on that toilet and push and wait. Wait until you're absolutely sure you can't wee any more."

I was trapped. My home had become my catacomb, wherein I was helpless, and Annie was pulling all the strings like I was her Marionette puppet. I was late for work this particular morning. I called in saying that I had over slept, when I had actually spent over an hour sitting on the toilet. But hey, as a result of all this hard work I'd lost another ¼ lb, dropping to my tinniest yet. WELL DONE JOANNE! A teeny tiny 108 pounds: 7 stone and 9 pounds! This may not sound particularly low to you if you have an eating disorder yourself, but to me, it was my biggest achievement in life to date - MY LOWEST weight EVER! *This* was something that I could finally excel at. What I didn't realise was that as I had been rushing around because I was late, I had only put on my size eight trousers, which by now had started to hang off me. Somehow, I had forgotten to put on my thick tights, my leggings and the size ten trousers which were supposed to sit on top of these other three layers. People could now see just how much weight I'd actually lost over the past month.

Catacomb

That morning, I went through the security portal at work as normal; for those of you who haven't worked in a prison, this is most easily compared to an airport search. By now, this was just part of my daily routine. I was standing on the 'searching box' when the operational support grade who was frisking me chided "Jesus, Joanne, you're wasting away. How much weight have you lost? What diet is that? I really need to give it a go." Suddenly I realised that I could have actually blown Annie's disguise.

OH CRAP! How am I going to get myself out of this one? Faster than I could even say 'good morning', I replied! "No diet, I'm just training really, really hard as I want to be a Physical Education Instructor." Phew! It really is a good job I can think on my feet at times. The truth is I did use this ruse to my advantage many times over the next few years, because that conversation had introduced the idea of another thing that Annie could control - exercise. I started telling everyone that I wanted to become a PEI. At the time, I had just started working on the Juvenile Unit, which gave me the opportunity to train even harder than I would have been able to if I'd been working anywhere else in the jail. I even started a physical education diary to record all my activities, as part of my wanting-to-be-a-PEI subterfuge. At one point I was training up to four hours a day, before and after work and then at lunch. We were also actively encouraged to take part in activities with our Juvenile offenders, and I would always be the staff member to opt for the gym sessions. What I didn't take in to account was that all this sport actually made me gain more weight, because muscle weighs heavier than fat.

Diary entry: April 22nd, 2006: I really want to go to the gym again tonight, I feel guilty as fuck! My throat is sore from all the purging! Gym done, then more exercise afterwards at home equals no more binging! I'm an amazing actress. I make everyone believe that I'm happy when I'm not. I don't care about healthy; I just need to be skinny.

Bizarrely, amid all this food-hate and lack of control, I began to enjoy cooking. I guess the attraction was two-fold. Firstly, the preparation of nice dishes offered me the illusion of control. Often, I would be overcome by an uncontrollable urge to binge on whatever was at hand. If I planned and prepared my food, I could kid myself that I was being 'normal'. And weirdly, I did actually enjoy nice food. I loved eating out but I couldn't risk it when Annie was in full swing, because I might not be able to get to the toilet in time, so I preferred to eat at home. My binge foods tended to be bland, soft and starchy, so the chance to experiment with different tastes and textures was a luxury. Secondly, I loved to please. I was desperate for people to like me, and I soon found out that they seemed to enjoy my cooking. I was like one of those 'Feeders' who take pleasure in providing for others. Did I also think that if *they* ate more, *I* wouldn't be the only fat one? I'm not sure whether I analysed it to that degree. When my friends wanted to get together, it was much easier to invite them over to my house, where I could be in control, than to risk going out. One of my specialities was my cheesecakes. Actually here, my passion and my hate collided, as they did make an easy binge food too when the need overwhelmed me.

June 7th, 2006

It was a PEI called Darren from work who was the first person to realise just how ill I really was. We had become friends when I first started working at Ribbleton, and we wound each other up something chronic, by playing practical jokes on one another. He would go on leave and return to work to find that his mug had been set in jelly in the gym fridge or his belongings had been hidden around the gym with a trail of clues so he could find them via a treasure hunt. He did get his revenge on me once, when he was looking after my flat while I was away; I came home to find that all my furniture had been tipped upside down and all my drawers had been rearranged. What once belonged in the kitchen was now in the bathroom or bedrooms. Oh, and the pebbles from my coffee table had been hidden all over the house (I was still finding these over three years later!). When Darren had heard that I was interested in becoming a PEI, he had offered to train with me and help me to reach my goal!

After one particularly hard spinning session in the gym one lunch time, we were both working overtime on House Unit One. I was standing on the Wing, supervising Association (prisoners' recreation time) when Darren asked me how on earth I managed to eat so much crap and yet stay so thin. He really caught me off guard with this direct question and I clearly wasn't thinking straight when I answered him. Although I used a flippant tone, and didn't expect him to take me seriously, as soon as I said I would just throw it up again later I knew I had unmasked Annie. My secret had slipped out. I saw his face change and although I tried to laugh it off, it was too late: the damage had already been done. Darren grabbed me by the arm and pulled me in to the wing office, slamming the door shut behind us. I knew there was no way of me getting out of this one, there was no amount back peddling that could undo the words that had just escaped my lips!

I explained to him that this wasn't the time or place for this conversation to take place. Secretly, I was hoping that he would forget all about what I'd just said, but deep down inside I knew that it wouldn't be left there, because not only was Darren my colleague and friend, but he was also one of my neighbours at the time. I was right. He arrived at my flat about 7pm carrying a handful of leaflets from a local eating disorder group called Caraline, and in that minute I realised that there was no escaping his involvement. Maybe, in fact, my prayers for someone to help me had finally been answered.

I invited Darren in and made us each a cup of coffee before I headed back into the lounge to talk to him. I would have preferred something stronger, but I feared more disapproval. Before even taking one sip of his drink, Darren urged "Joanne, either you elect to get some help yourself, or I will make you get the help you need and the choice will be taken away from you." Funny choice that. Admit you have a problem and deal with it, or be made to deal with it anyway. I didn't have a problem . . . me . . . no way.

MYSELF, ME AND I

I was in complete control, I knew exactly what I was doing, and I could take it or leave it. Somehow, when cornered, I actually believed this nonsense. Joanne was in control. Despite my continued bluffing (to myself as well as to Darren), I promised to answer his questions honestly.

1. How long have you been doing this for?
Almost fifteen years, since I was twelve years old.

2. How many times a day do you binge?
Anything up to ten times a day.

3. How do you binge?
I used to have to stick my fingers down my throat, but now most of the time I only have to think about it and it happens. I also use laxatives and exercise as additional purge methods.

4. How many laxatives a day do you take?
I started out small, but now I am up to about 60 a day.

5. What is your average food intake in any one binge sitting?
That all depends on the binge.

6. OK then, what is the worst binge that you can ever remember?
(I didn't even have to think about this answer!)
A full bucket of KFC Family Size, complete with all the trimmings, a packet of custard

creams, followed by a large tub of ice cream. All washed down with two litres of Pepsi.

7. What types of food are your usual binge foods?
Ice cream, donuts, biscuits, MacDonald's, pizza, sausage rolls, anything I can get my hands on really, when I need to binge, the food is not important, it's the binge that is.

8. Does anyone else know about your bulimia?
No. I've never told anyone, apart from my dead friend Jennie.

9. What's the worst thing that you can ever remember doing to satisfy a binge? (It took me a while to answer this question, and I asked Darren if he really wanted to know the answer. He assured me he did!)
I've eaten food from out of the bin!

By the end of the last question, the look left on Darren's face was one of sheer pity. I wondered if this might lessen his righteous approach to my problem, but somehow I knew he was deadly serious. This wasn't some kind of idle threat. Either I did this with his help or he would take action to make me get the help I needed. I knew he meant well and that he genuinely believed that he could help me, but as you probably know, no one can really make someone do what they don't want to do, until they are ready to take ownership of their issues. Nothing was really going to change (except my liberty) because I wasn't yet ready to face this war with Annie.

I did battle on, trying to keep Annie at bay, and Darren's daily visits to check my cupboards for 'binge foods' did massively reduce my binges. He also confiscated my weighing scales. After another two weeks, he came over with a hammer in his hand and made me follow him down to my parking space. In the empty space sat my glass weighing scales with a white piece of paper folded up on top of them. I looked at him quizzically before walking over to pick up the piece of paper. I unfolded it to see that Darren had written "I am not a slave to my weight." I smiled, thinking if only it were that simple. Darren handed me the hammer and told me to smash the scales to pieces. I did so, but only because it was easier to appease him than to argue with him. Darren continued to do the best he could to monitor me, but I was always one step ahead of him. Don't forget I was an expert in deception; I'd been doing this for many years now. I found new hiding places around the house and hid my newly purchased set of scales in a pillow slip with my spare bedding. Once again, I was like a child at home, hiding things away in secret, only this time I was an adult living in my own home, under constant scrutiny.

Diary entry: June 25th, 2006: My world is such a cruel, harsh place. Why do I feel like shit? I don't think Google could even give me an answer! I'm tired of feeling so numb and now I have the added pressure of being under a microscope again, forever scrutinised, my cupboards looked in every day and my scales taken away! Think that you can stop me? We're smarter than that! But I am my own worst enemy, I criticise you, I hurt you, I scare you, I make you cry, I am your mind and I am slowly killing you.

Shortly after Darren started his I-can-save-Joanne mission, I was over at Becky's one evening relaxing and having a good old catch up, when she announced that we should put together a dating profile for me. I suspiciously asked her why she would want to do that, protesting (while laughing) that surely I wasn't that hard up just yet. Moments later, Becky had her camera out and was soon leaping around her lounge trying to take my picture as I ducked and twisted and threw cushions at her, telling her to quit because I always took a horrible picture. She carried on, and I gave up, telling her sarcastically to go ahead if she must!

I had forgotten all about this until the next time I saw Becky, which was when she revealed that she had written a profile and posted it on Sarah Beeny's site 'My Single Friend'. I laughed, and wasn't at all sure how to respond to her protestations that I was too nice to be single and deserved to have someone in my life. I asked to have a look; this is what Becky posted:

Joanne has been a very good friend of mine for a few years now, and is a thoughtful, caring and loyal person who always has time for anyone. Joanne enjoys being outdoors, from walking to horse riding. She is well travelled and a regular jet setter, her holidays vary from exploring, to action packed, through to chilling out and relaxing in hot places. Joanne will holiday anywhere, she has had many holidays abroad and in this country during the time I have known her and she always has her next trip planned.

Joanne is extremely hard working and strives to achieve in her job. Her motivation for her hard work is probably the reason for her many holidays around the world and her vast designer shoe collection! Plus her well furnished and looked after home.

Joanne is a homely person and an extremely good and inventive cook, her culinary skills are to 'die' for. Joanne is very sociable and I would describe her as being able 'to take her anywhere' she adapts to suit any social occasion or function and is always presentable in dress, attitude and behaviour. Joanne is a very outgoing person who likes eating out, outdoor pursuits, and holidaying (as mentioned before), socialising in a pub or club, and is also known to like a night in, with a glass or two of wine.

Joanne exercises regularly to keep fit, and looks after herself! So would need a like minded person. The reason I believe Joanne is single is because she has not met Mr Right yet! Hopefully she will soon, so she can enjoy all of her many interests with him.

I mentioned the holidays before, but I haven't mentioned the designer shoes, have I? What can I say? It's logical if you give it some thought. I was deeply unhappy with my appearance and had spent thousands on trying to improve what I looked like by changing my body shape. I refused to go anywhere without makeup. Of course I would enjoy spending my money on material things as well as on emotional distractions, and if those material things could make me look better at the same time, then they were an obvious investment, weren't they? Particularly if it meant people would be looking at my feet instead of other parts of my body!

Becky's words were so complimentary that it was impossible to be annoyed with her. I was moved that she actually thought these things about me. I was so convinced that people didn't think positively about me. I was touched that she obviously liked me so much, more, in fact, than I liked myself. During the drive home, and back at the flat later that evening, I thought about what Becky had written. I decided to take a chance and do something which I would normally never have done. I logged onto the dating site, thinking "What's the worst that can happen?"

August 17th, 2006

I had met John online in June, and we had started dating. I'd arranged to go out for an Indian meal with my friends for my birthday but I was quite anxious about the whole event. I was meeting up with all my closest friends including Joy, Becky, Emma, Darren, and their partners. It was the first time that any of them would meet the new guy I had started seeing thanks to Becky's dating advert. I was concerned both about what they would think of John, and also because I had put on some weight due to being watched like a hawk by Darren. I also knew that, with the people I was going to be out with, I would end up drinking quite a bit. John had not yet met drunk Joanne! But after a few glasses of wine I started to relax, the food we ate was lovely and everyone was having such a good time. I guess I must let my guard down a little too much, because after eating my dinner, as everyone else was chatting or dancing to the live jazz band that was playing, off I went to the bathroom, not realizing Darren had been watching me and had seen me sneak away. I did my purge and as I left the toilets, there he was, just outside the Ladies', glaring at me. I walked passed him and to the bar to get a drink, but he came up behind me and whispered in my ear "You have a week to tell them, or I will!" I spun round and begged him not to make me do it. "One week!" he repeated, and I could see in his eyes that he was serious.

As the night went on, everyone was in good spirits and having a great time. The drinks flowed, but I couldn't relax anymore. I received a text message each day for the next five days asking if I had told them yet. On day five, I went over to see Darren to try to reason with him. "Joanne," he declared, "I promised I would try to help you, but I've realised that I can't do that alone. Your friends care about you and they need to know. It is only right; they will help you more than I can on my own." I begged and pleaded with him not to make me do this, but he meant what he had said. I felt like I was trapped in a corner and I had no more Get Out of Jail Free cards left, so later that evening, I reluctantly went over to see Becky. As I sat and told her, she just looked at me with that same pitiful expression that Darren had. What she said surprised me though: "But why? You are one of the strongest women I know, you're thin and you're beautiful, you own your own home, you travel the world, and have the most amazing vast designer shoe collection! You are confident, bubbly and the life and soul of any party! I don't get it . . . *why?*" So I told Becky some of my story. A few days later it was Emma's turn, but she wasn't shocked at all. She said it explained lots of things and now everything made total sense to her.

So there we had it, my two closest local friends knew about Annie and some of why and how she had come to be. I was actually more relieved than I thought I would be at first, because I guess deep down I was so tired of fighting this all alone. But I still hadn't quite hit rock bottom. All my friends rallied around, supporting me. I know they wanted to help fight my battles, and believed that they genuinely could help, but the reality was that I felt smothered, and so I withdrew into myself even more.

Diary entry: September 6th, 2006: I'm an ugly bitch! I don't deserve friends! I hate lying to everyone. I'm stupid, fat, ugly and lumpy. Underachiever, bad friend, bad daughter. Ew, I SUCK! I would love to know what runs through people's minds when they think of me. I love how everyone who knows about my eating disorder thinks they can help me, like it's their fault I'm ill. It's my fault I'm fat, not yours . . .

Naturally, I had to tell John too, and believe me this honesty didn't help our relationship, which was pretty turbulent. Of course we had some good times, but we had plenty of bad times too. John was so controlling, and the knowledge of my problems provided him with the ideal weapon to control me with.

I became more secretive and simply told each person what I felt they wanted to hear. "Yes it's been a good day. I haven't binged once today." There were days when this was true, but on others it wasn't. I felt trapped by their constant supervision; I felt they were always watching me, assessing how long I was in the bathroom. When I *was* in the bathroom there was often someone waiting for me outside. All in case I purged. But of course the purge was just the symptom, not the cause. I had to look at this in another way if I was to beat them. I needed something to stop me overeating in the first place, something that would suppress my appetite. I discovered diet pills.

I was told that the pills would suppress my appetite and would help me to train longer and harder in the gym, while speeding up my metabolism. To me, they were the most amazing thing I had ever heard of. They could cure all my problems and stop me overeating? Why hadn't I heard of these before?! Probably, it was because they weren't legal (I didn't know, or suspect, this at the time, but these innocent little pills contained ephedrine). So I paid my £25 for 100 of these little white miracle workers. I was told to take two tablets an hour before my breakfast and two more an hour before my lunch for the best results. I was never to take them after 3pm as they could affect my sleeping. Still no alarm bells were ringing, even at this point.

The first that day I took the tablets I remember feeling spaced out and very thirsty. I didn't like how they made me feel, but I had no appetite at all, so I didn't binge or feel like binging for the first time in as long as I could remember. Strangely, maybe because of whatever was in them, or maybe because I finally felt as if Annie could be kept at bay, I felt very confident in myself. These feelings didn't last very long, however, and I was soon upping the dosage so that I could feel this way again. I began to not sleep well, and my mind was always on overdrive, racing at about a hundred miles an hour, thinking about things that I didn't need to think about. I couldn't switch my thoughts off. Still not suspecting my new found diet pills were the cause of these problems, I eventually went to see my doctor who put my insomnia down to shift work, and informed me that lots of prison and police officers, nurses, etc have bouts of sleeplessness at some point. She prescribed a seven day course of Diazepam to bring my sleeping pattern back on track.

The Diazepam didn't work, so when I visited again, the doctor gave me a stronger dose. I was starting to be concerned because through my job I was aware of the nature of this type of drug, and the fact that it could be very addictive. I decided only to take one every three or four days, by which time I was so exhausted that I really couldn't function anymore. I didn't want to get hooked on sleeping medication, but this routine wasn't working for me, so I went back to see the doctor again, asking for something less addictive. My doctor finally became concerned when three months after my first visit I still wasn't sleeping well. She began investigating the possible causes, but couldn't find any explanation, so she referred me to a sleep clinic in Cambridge. During the sleep experiment, it was discovered that I wasn't going into REM sleep, which meant I didn't go in to a deep sleep. I was actually asleep for just 48 minutes the whole night. No wonder I was constantly exhausted.

Not long after this, Becky was on a diet herself and struggling to lose weight, so I told her about my amazing diet pills. It was only then I discovered what I was actually putting in to my body. "Joanne, you know they contain amphetamines don't you?" I couldn't believe it, but Becky reassured me she was serious and then picked up her laptop to show me exactly what I was taking. And I'd been worried about the Diazepam! I couldn't believe that I had been so stupid. I was a prison officer and I was putting illegal substances in my body. What an idiot! As I sat reading the list of side effects, including sleep issues, heart palpitations and paranoia I felt so stupid and naive for not thinking about what I was doing to myself. I instantly stopped taking the pills and flushed what was left down the toilet. But, as soon as I did this, BANG! Annie was back again, as though she'd simply had a little summer vacation.

Diary entry: January 11th, 2007: I wish I could stop, I know I'm drinking too much. I want to stop. I'm not joking, but it hurts too much to deal with the pain inside. Why was I born? I'm the fat friend, if you feel fat then stand by me because you will look thin. Is this why people invite me out? I feel like someone is holding my head under water so that I can just drown in a sorrow of self hate.

Diary entry: July 18th, 2007: How long do I have to put up with this pain before the inevitable happens?

I don't love him. I don't think I ever did. I can't even stand to have sex with him any more unless it's in the shower so that I can wash myself clean again straight away. There's a smile on my face even though my heart is frowning. But what do I say when people ask me how I am? I'M FINE . . .

February, 2008

Diary entry: February 1st, 2008: I'm scared of myself and my mind! Stop shouting at me Annie; you're killing me right now. Look at what I've become because of you! But yet I still listen to you! I think about food all day, every day. Should I eat it, or should I not eat it. Should I take some laxatives or save them for another day? When you're in doubt, lax it out . . .

The last year and a half had been a blur of arguments and promises, of binging and alcohol, of stress and sleeplessness. The diet pills had knocked my sleeping pattern right out and I couldn't seem to get it back on track. I was binging and purging in secret again and I still wasn't sleeping well. I wasn't getting along with my line manager at work, and she seemed to be doing her best to block me from getting a promotion at every opportunity. I was still drinking far too much and my relationship was turbulent (to say the least).

John and I were engaged and were even planning a wedding, but as soon as we managed a few positive steps forward we always seemed to have a fight, usually over something trivial. The constant yo-yoing was so tiresome, but I simply accepted this as my

147

lot. In fact, I'm not sure accepted is accurate, as that implies that it was a conscious decision. Actually it was more like I just existed from day to day. There were *some* highlights; we had a couple of great holidays (John had actually proposed in Jamaica) but in reality, trying to fight for the relationship was so tiring in itself. I was so exhausted but I couldn't sleep and I was easily irritated by John's snoring, but if I ventured to the sofa or the spare room, it caused yet another argument because apparently I didn't love him if I didn't want to sleep with him! I tried everything I could think of from ear plugs to sleeping tablets, but they weren't really helping. All I needed, all I craved, was a good night's sleep. ARRRGGGGHHHHHH!

Diary entry: February 13th, 2008: I feel like I'm living the worst day over and over again, stuck on repeat. Every day is the worst day ever. My thoughts really disturb me sometimes. I just want to be happy! I wonder if I will still be alive by then? I really only just want to be happy; I wonder what that actually feels like. Maybe they sell it on eBay! I know I'm just being an overly emotional hormonal dumbass.

I then went on to invest a lot of money into John's new business venture because it was a good idea and I really wanted it to work out for him (for us). I even tried to help him promote the business in my spare time. One way that I did this was to send a few emails at work to some of my friends and colleagues, telling them about a current competition that was being run. However, my line manager immediately collared me about this, waving a copy of the code of discipline at me while warning that I could 'lose my job' over this transgression. It had been a genuine mistake and I never would have sent the emails if I had known how much trouble they could get me into. My manager advised me to recall the messages that I had sent, and then said I was a "Stupid idiot!" as I had included the Security Governor on the circulation list. She said that this meant that it would probably go to a full investigation and that I would be lucky to keep my job. I had no idea that I had put any Governors on the distribution list and I tried to recall the message as advised. When that didn't work, I thought I would go and see the Security Governor in person, hold my hands up and take a slap on the wrist, hoping that my apology would somewhat lesson the blow that I had coming my way. For three days I tried to speak to him, for three days I walked along that long corridor of power, feeling like I was walking the Green Mile to my execution. For three long days I knocked on his blue door but there was no answer. "Life, I beg you, please give me a break. I'm not a bad person really, or at least I try not to be, so please just cut me a little slack! Just for once."

That evening, I arrived home to become embroiled in yet another row that I knew would inevitably be twisted and end up my fault, as always. I stood up to walk away from the disagreement because I couldn't be bothered with it anymore. I was so tired of everything. As I got into the hallway, John shouted something that finally, after almost three years, made me snap and fight back. "That's it. You fuck off. Go on, fuck off and don't bother to come back!" I spun around so that I was now facing him. I was livid. How dare *he* tell *me* to fuck off and not come back! "It's my fucking house!" I screamed at him.

I then spotted the sky remote which was hurtling towards my head (being a cricketer, I knew John had a fantastic aim!), but I didn't have time to dodge it and besides I was now so angry and pumped full of adrenaline that I wasn't going to. I think I had also put myself into shock because I was finally standing up to him! Luckily the remote just missed me, smashing into the wall to the left of my head. John then got up, barged past me out of the house and slammed the door behind him. Suddenly, I physically crashed and had no energy left. All that remained as John stormed away from the house was a nothingness, an emptiness. I had now hit rock bottom.

I gathered myself up, shaking like a leaf, and walked to the shop to buy the first packet of cigarettes in as long as I could remember, along with a bottle of Jack Daniels. When I got back home, I loaded my CD player with my favourite Pink Floyd album (probably not the best idea in the world when you're already feeling really low!), and poured myself a large drink.

I then sat on the sofa assessing my life. I looked around at the lovely flat I had created and thought about the pain that I'd experienced there. It hadn't been the sanctuary it was supposed to be. My own problems had of course, followed me, and then more had come into the mix, my 'helpful' but intrusive friends and my destructive relationship with John. I found myself staring at the bag of sleeping tablets which I had picked up the day before. Sitting in a plastic bag on the coffee table was a three month supply. In that moment, I wondered how easy it would be to pop them one by one into my mouth and simply go to sleep and never have to wake up again, to go to sleep and feel nothing, no more pain, no more hurt and no more self loathing!

Knocking back glass after glass of the Jack Daniels, I thought "I can't take this anymore. Who knew my life could be so frightening? It's DO or DIE now Joanne." Somewhere inside me, the person that I hadn't yet become was yelling "Do, Do, Do," but Joanne, was yelling "Die, Die, Die," while Annie, of course, had to take centre stage; taunting us both and flaunting her lack of care, *her* lack of consequence. While Me and I argued, Annie sang the same verse over and over again like a child: "Ring-a-Ring-a-Rosies, A Pocket full of Posies, A-tishoo! A-tishoo! - WE ALL FALL DOWN!"

It was in those dark moments that I spoke to Jennie for the first time in over six years, apologising for my lack of sympathy for her actions: "Jennie, if you felt half of what I am feeling in this moment, I now understand, because I'm afraid, I'm alone, and I don't know what to do anymore. Please help me!" I then finally made my peace with her and I forgave her. I'm not really sure what happened after that; I must have passed out in yet another drunken coma.

All I need is a Hug

I came to at 4.45am, still on the sofa, still in my uniform and feeling very hung-over.

I climbed into the shower pondering what I had done so wrong in this life, or maybe a previous one, to have been dealt such shit. How the hell does this happen to a 29 year old woman? I was in a relationship that made me truly miserable, I'd made a genuine mistake at work which might have cost me the job I loved, my immediate boss was being horrible to me for no apparent reason and I was so unhappy with myself, that I would rather be dead than carry on this miserable existence! Of course it didn't occur to me at the time that I was effectively a shit-magnet: I might have had my party-girl mask, but given my true feelings about myself, how could I possibly have had a healthy, happy relationship or attracted positive experiences? With the shower still running, I sat down in the bath and pulled my knees up to my chest, encircling my arms around them and held myself tightly, with the warm water beating down on my skin.

I heard the alarm sound on my mobile phone. This meant that it was now 6.30am. I had been sitting in the shower for almost two hours! I'm not sure how long I would have stayed in there if the alarm hadn't gone off. I unclasped my arms and stood up, slowly coming out of the daze. Wrapping a towel around myself I headed to the lounge to switch off my phone. As I picked the phone up, I saw that I had three missed calls and at least half a dozen text messages. I didn't have the energy to look at them. I headed instead to the kitchen to make myself a strong coffee before I faced John's angry reaction to the previous night's argument. As I expected, there was a torrent of abuse, but there was also a text from Becky: "Are you OK? I'm worried about you. Please call me. I've tried three times to ring you and no answer." Some memory stirred, and I checked my sent items; right at the top was "Hey, Bec, can you come over I REALLY need a HUG!" I sent her a quick message apologising, explaining briefly that John and I had had yet another fight, and telling her I would see her later.

It was a cold and frosty February morning, but I felt the need for fresh air and decided to walk to work so I could clear my head. As I was walking, my phone beeped in my pocket with a new message from Becky. "How much more of this shit are you going to put up with? You deserve much, much better than to be treated like this! I'm not in today but I'll speak to you later. Love ya x." I knew she was right. I knew everyone was right, and I knew I wanted out of the relationship, but I didn't know if I had the strength to do it. I laughed to myself before responding with. "It's *your* fault I ended up with him, ha-ha!" Damn Sarah Beeny's dating site! Seconds later, my phone beeped again! "I know SORRY, SORRY, SORRY, SORRY, SORRY XXXXXXXX!" At least that put a smile on my face for a while. I arrived at work and went up to the locker room. I grabbed my utility belt, put back on my trusted empty smile, and headed to the gate pretending that everything was alright, as always.

I went through staff search and collected my keys and radio before heading up to the corridor of power for the fourth time in one week. As I climbed the stairs, the knot in my stomach grew tighter and tighter. Finally I reached top. I couldn't do it, not today. I had enough to contend with already. I quickly spun back around and retreated down the stairs and up to House Unit Six. The morning dragged by so slowly, and as I headed to the gym at lunchtime, I decided that I didn't even have the energy for a workout today. Knowing I was just putting off the inevitable, and thinking I may as well get all my shit dealt with at the same time rather than just prolonging the agony, I decided to sort out the email issue so that at least *that* would be out of the way, and if I did have more shit to deal with, if I did have to lose my job, then it may as well happen now.

I knocked on the blue door yet again, but there was still no answer! I tried a second time, but nothing. I spotted a member of the security department further down the corridor and asked him if he knew where Ian was. I was told he was with the Deputy Governor. Taking a huge breath, I headed in that direction, determined to get this over and done with *now*. The Deputy Governor's door was slightly ajar. I knocked, and was invited in. The Deputy Governor asked me what she could do for me and I explained that I actually needed to talk to Ian when he was free. I was so scared my heart felt like it was going to explode; it was beating incredibly fast, and my mouth felt dry, just like sand paper. "Sure Joanne." Ian said "I'll see you in my office in a minute." I forced a smile and walked back towards his office, realising there was no going back now.

I opened Ian's office door and stepped inside, leaving the door open while I waited. The few minutes I stood alone, my mind was racing. After all these attempts to see him, I wasn't even prepared! I didn't know what I was going to say or how I was going to say it. I was more petrified than I had ever been in my life! Ian was the Head of Security; I hadn't had much to do with him since I'd been at the prison and didn't know much about him. I had no idea what to expect. I was so used to thinking negatively about myself and I was used to thinking that other people must think of me negatively too, but I still had some sense of justice. I knew I was good at my job, and it was unfair that a stupid but genuine mistake could put that at risk. What had I done?! A few minutes later, Ian walked in and closed the door behind him. As he headed to his desk, I was frozen to the spot in fear. When he turned to face me and asked what he could do for me, I couldn't answer. I tried to speak, but nothing came out. "Joanne," he asked "Are you OK?" Then the verbal diarrhoea hit, and in a panicked tone, I stammered. "I sent you an email, I never meant to, I tried to recall it but I couldn't. I'm sorry. I've been told I could lose my job because it's against the prison service rules. It was an accident and I really am sorry." I burst into tears as I finished the last word. I was never emotional like this at work, but it was as if the floodgates had been finally opened, and I couldn't control myself, never mind actually stop.

MYSELF, ME AND I

This wasn't just a woman crying, I was a hysterical wreck. I have never cried like this in my life. I couldn't breathe, and began to hyperventilate. I was completely out of control, but still aware of Ian, standing in front of his desk, looking . . . Erm . . . lost! If I could sketch the image he would have a cartoon speech bubble coming from his mouth, with the words "Shit! Hysterical woman! Where the hell are the tissues?!"

The next thing I knew, he just walked over to me and threw his arms around me. Holding me tightly, because I was crying so very hard. In those few moments, it was almost as though this man, who didn't know me, became my sponge. Suddenly, all those years of negative feelings, of hate and self loathing were being absorbed from me, and for the first time I felt a genuine warmth. I felt safe in his arms. All I had wanted for so very long was someone just to throw their arms around me and tell me that everything would be OK.

When I finally managed to compose myself, I reluctantly pulled myself away and apologised. I had never expected the hug I had so longed for to come from a stranger, but somehow now it made total sense. Of course, my friends and family were always giving me hugs, but those were different. This man, this stranger, knew nothing about me or my problems and yet he did the one thing I needed the most, at the very point in my life when it mattered the most. For whatever reason, that hug made me see things in a whole new light. Ian spoke to me again. "Joanne, what on earth was all that about?" "The email, I really am sorry!" He turned around and walked over to his desk, sat down to log on to his computer and then found and deleted my email. He looked at me with a gentle smile and asked "What email?" I managed a smile back before saying thank you. "Joanne," he continued, I've never seen you like that; are you sure that was all over an email?" I nodded my head and again apologised, thinking if only you knew, if only anyone knew. But until the first person read the draft of the book you're reading now, no one had any idea of the true amount of pain I was hiding.

As I left Ian's office, I saw things so clearly for the first time; it was as if that hug had flipped on a light switch. I saw Joanne, with Annie so close by, and I realised that things were finally going to change. I walked into Ian's office as Me, as Joanne. I walked out as I, as Jo. Joanne had somehow disappeared inside that hug. It was what I had needed to release her, to say goodbye to the scared and unhappy little girl that I had been for so very long. Now I had a sense of clarity and could see my future for the very first time. That hug had planted the seeds of the beginning, of my new life.

I headed to the Ladies' because I knew my face would be red from crying. Luckily, I had been on the early shift, so I was actually able to go straight home, knowing that at least I would have a couple of hours to myself before I'd have to face John again, assuming he bothered to come home. I sat down on my familiar sofa feeling so very different from the last time I had sat there. Had that really only been the night before? I felt amazing warmth which seemed to bring with it a certainty that I could beat this. I didn't have to put up with this life any more. I grabbed the bottle of Jack Daniels from the coffee table, walked to the kitchen sink, and poured what was left away. Then I threw the remainder of the pack of cigarettes in to the bin.

The front door opened at 6pm, and in John walked. I told him I needed to ask him a question and asked him to sit down. "Do you trust me?" I waited in silence for a reply. Obviously the question was too complicated! "Do you trust me when I tell you that looking at those pro-anorexia sites doesn't encourage me to binge? Do you trust me in general?"

I looked him straight in the eye and waited for what seemed like an eternity before he replied. "No, Jo, I don't." John stood up and left the house again, but this time there was no fear and worry trailing after him. Instead, I felt relief, as if a weight had been lifted from my shoulders. I knew now that I had the strength to finally let him go. I felt nothing; no anger, no guilt and no longing. I didn't want him and I didn't need him after all. I felt just a sense of release and tranquillity.

I called Becky (the phone rang only once before she answered), and asked if I could stay with her for a few days. I grabbed my car keys and headed out the door. I felt so calm, so strong, so liberated! This was something I'd never experienced before. I felt so warm and free! I arrived at Becky's about fifteen minutes later; I didn't even have time to knock on the door before she opened it. "What on earth is going on?" she asked. I smiled, "It's done, and I'm done!" I walked into the house, spun round and gave Becky a huge hug. "I really mean it." She stared at me, before finding the words, "What on earth has got in to you? I've never seen you like this! I've never seen you look like you do, but I don't actually know what's different about you!" "Get me a glass of wine, I need to celebrate!" I followed her in to the kitchen "Celebrate? You're really serious, aren't you?" I had the biggest Cheshire grin on my face. "Yes, deadly serious!" "So what's changed? I do think you know, that you're doing the right thing in ending the relationship. Don't you?" she asked, before throwing her arms around me again.

Becky poured a glass of wine for me and a whiskey and diet coke for herself, I raised my glass. "Here's a toast!" and we clinked our glasses together "But what are we toasting?" Becky asked. "We're toasting the start of my new life." She was inevitably confused. I explained that it was time to let everything go and to "Sort my shit out." Becky looked at me sceptically and said she really hoped so, "You are such a great person; I just wish you would believe me." I smiled, and asked her to promise one thing before we went any further: "Never write me an online dating profile or attempt to sort my love life out again, because if you do you are on a friendship ban."

We both burst out laughing and headed into the lounge to sit down. Becky sat staring at me with a smile on her face, "So come on, who are you? And where is my friend Joanne?" I assured her she was looking at the new and improved me, that this was the Jo she had better get used to from now on. I told

159

her I was going to sort everything out, the lot: the eating, the self loathing, the binge drinking, I was even going to stop caring about what people thought about me. Becky just laughed, "Yeah right, OK, as she sits there with a large glass of wine." I picked it up "This doesn't count, this is a celebration!" I protested, taking another sip. "So why now, and what has changed?" Becky asked again. "I made myself look a complete tit at work today. I burst in to tears on a Suit, Becky. I'm not talking a *little* cry either, I was inconsolable!" Becky just laughed again. "Don't . . . I'm so embarrassed, but he just gave me a hug, a real bear hug. I honestly don't think he knew what else to do with me! Becky, I am talking mascara, snot, tears the lot, all over his shirt sleeve!" "Oh my God, Jo! You are so funny. But if you mean what you're saying about finally wanting to sort everything out, it was a good thing and I'm glad it happened." "I know, so am I! I've never felt like this before, I feel totally . . ." I paused for a minute, thinking of the right words to say. "Totally what, Jo?" ". . . alive, alive for the first time! I sound bonkers, don't I?" "Yes you do, but I still love you! Now come here and give me some of that alive-goodness!" I popped my glass on the table and gave Becky another hug.

I went back into the kitchen, grabbed my phone and returned to the sofa. As I started composing a text, Becky frowned and asked quizzically "What are you doing now?" I explained that I was sending John a message to let him know that I was done, that *we* were done. I told him I'd gone away for a few days so that he could sort his things out. I didn't even hesitate before hitting, send. I didn't want to talk to him, I was through with talking. I just wanted to start getting on with the rest of my life.

I headed towards the kitchen again. "Now what on earth are you doing?" With a mischievous smile, I told a flabbergasted Becky that I was going into her garden to do a cartwheel! She asked if I had already had a drink before I arrived at her house. "Nope, I drove here and I've only had those two sips from the glass you gave me. I'm just drunk on life this evening! I have a random urge to do a cartwheel and do a cartwheel I will, just because I can!" Becky followed me into the garden, still laughing. She continued to laugh as I continued attempting to do cartwheels! I finally gave this up as a bad job after the third attempt.

I slept so very well that night, so peacefully, that I only woke when my alarm rang. I couldn't remember the last time I had slept so soundly. Unfortunately, it suddenly dawned on me that I had not brought my uniform with me and that I'd have to go back home to get it. A little panicked by this thought, I asked Becky if she would come with me.

I wasn't sure what awaited me at home, and had all kinds of things racing through my mind. Would my house have been trashed? Would John still be there? Would there be trouble if he was? Even in my now good mood, I began to panic. I knew this is what I really wanted, but I was still petrified and also a little angry as I realised that I should never have to feel scared about being in my own home. As we got closer to home, Becky could see that I was getting more and more nervous, and reassured me that I was fine, that I wasn't alone, and that I could do this. I knew she was right, but I was still worried; I couldn't help the way I was feeling inside. We climbed the stairs to my flat and I put my key slowly into the front door, reluctant to open it. But I had nothing to fear: the house was exactly as I had left it. I quickly threw on my uniform, feeling that I should leave as soon as I could, but I suddenly had a strong urge to check John's wardrobe. I held the handles and gently pulled the doors towards me. As they opened, I could see that all of his belongings were gone. Once again, I felt a strong sense of relief and contentment that this part of my life was finally coming to an end. I stayed with Becky for few more days. Her partner was working nights anyway, and I needed some company for a while. I finally returned home on the Saturday. It was a little strange at first being alone in the house, but as I climbed into my freshly made bed at about 10pm that night, I thought simply "Hello bed, I love you!" That night I slept better than I had in over three years, not rising for over thirteen hours, until sometime after 11am on the Sunday morning.

Returning to work on Monday, I was reminded of the previous Thursday and my hysterical outburst. I needed to apologise again to Ian. I was feeling acutely embarrassed and didn't know what to say. I sat staring at my computer with a blank mind. After a long ten minutes, I finally managed a brief email: "Hi Ian, I am really sorry for bursting in to tears on you last Thursday. I'm sure the last thing you expected when you walked into work was some hysterical woman breaking down in front of you. Thanks again for your help. Jo." I wasn't expecting a reply, but later that day I received the following "Hi Jo, no apology needed, my ears are always open should you need them! Ian." I didn't know it yet, but later that week I *would* need Ian's help again.

By the Monday evening, I was fed up and frustrated. John had been sending me revolting text messages, which I had been trying very hard not to respond to. I understood that he was hurt and angry that I had ended the relationship and I guess he knew that this time I really meant it. The fact that I wasn't responding to all of his messages was in itself an indication of my gradual emotional detachment and his loss of power over me. I thought that it might be easier if he wasn't able to contact me at all. We'd already done so much talking about our relationship, going round and round in circles, that I thought a final break in contact would make it easier for us each to move on. I was (am) very forgiving and loyal (maybe to a fault sometimes), but when pushed to a certain point I snap and that's that, I'll walk away and there's no going back.

The next day, I decided to contact both my mobile phone provider and my landline provider and get new numbers. That should be an end to the abuse as John would simply not be able to get in touch with me, or so I naively thought! Then the emails started, both at home and at work. At first, I tried to be polite and to reason with him to stop, but soon I found I was answering his emails in a snappy and aggressive way myself, and my mood was beginning to affect my work. Then came three emails which made me realise that this couldn't continue, I had to do something.

Firstly, John threatened to send his company bankrupt, "There goes all your money." I knew this was just an idle threat because he had invested too much time and effort into the business; I was sure he wouldn't want to lose that himself.

Secondly, he threatened! "I'm sure your Governors would love to know about your eating disorder - bang goes your job." This *did* worry me. John had once threatened to tell my mum about my eating problems. A few days later (after yet another fight), I was staying with Mum when she received a text message and simply asked me "Is it true?" The look of heartbreak on her face as she read his cruel text was devastating and still haunts me.

The third and final blow was really the lowest of the low. John threatened to kill himself, stating that he knew why my best friend Jennie had done the same thing. He told me that he knew how she had felt because I was enough to drive anyone to suicide. When I couldn't get hold of him I ran out of work and drove firstly to his parent's house and then to his work place, because I couldn't bear the thought of living with something like that on my conscience. When I couldn't find him or get hold of him; I felt I had no option by then but to involve his sister, as she was the only person I could reach by phone. I was worried he would do something silly but also angry that he would have done this to me.

I had done all I could, and so went back to work, where I found a final email waiting for me. John's sister had managed to get hold of him and now he was taunting me. I could almost hear his laughter as he delighted in the fact that I had been so worried about him, but then, he reassured me that he would never end his own life over a 'piece of shit' like me.

I knew John was hurting, but enough was enough. I could never forgive those last two emails, and everything I once felt for him turned at this point to anger and hatred. But I didn't know what to do. All of my friends and family were used to us fighting, splitting up and then getting back together again. That when I emailed my friends Sarah and Ant to let them know that the relationship had ended (as we were due to visit them soon in the USA and had arranged a trip to Mexico for the four of us), Sarah responded to me saying that we'd be back together soon. But, I knew this time was different and too much damage had been done (I think my friends only started to believe me when I took my sister to the USA instead), but I too had been used to the familiar on-off relationship and I wasn't sure how to handle this latest unpleasant development.

What I did know was that I couldn't keep receiving emails like this at work. I read and reread the emails, hoping for inspiration. Eventually, I decided to ask for help. The most logical person to approach, who would have the clout I needed, was the Head of Security . . . Ian. I sent him a brief email asking him if he had meant what he said about his ears being open. Fortunately, he said the offer had been genuine and I arranged a meeting with him the following day, so along I trotted, to knock on that blue door once more and to again ask for help. As I entered, I promised with a smile that I wouldn't be bursting into tears on him this time. Ian gave me a deadpan look and replied "Don't you worry. I grabbed the tissues, just in case," at which point he grabbed a toilet roll from next to his computer! I couldn't help but laugh. I explained to him that I had asked to see him not only because of his offer, but also because of his position. I also felt strangely comfortable talking to him, which was unusual for me (I wasn't generally comfortable being myself around men). I explained the situation as fully and honestly as I could, omitting only the references to my eating disorder. I asked if I could log onto his computer and show him the emails I was receiving. I asked if they could be blocked and this was done, which was a huge relief.

I went on to explain that I had told John that I was coming to see the Security Governor and that I didn't want to hear from him again. Ian offered to involve the Police Liaison Officer, but I explained that at this stage I hoped I had done enough, but that I might have to consider that as my next step if things escalated, which was why I had wanted to make someone at work aware of these problems now. I then asked Ian what affect the bankruptcy of the business, should it happen, would have on my role at the prison. He asked me if I had completed a Conflict of Interest Vulnerability Declaration Form. I explained that I had, but that I was the Company Secretary and the business bank account was in joint names because I had invested so much into it. Ian advised that this wasn't a problem and that I should contact the bank. If I explained my situation, they would be able to put a block on the account so that we would *both* have to sign in order to withdraw funds. I should then contact Companies House and have my name removed as the Company Secretary, "Problem solved!" I was really grateful for this advice, and thanked Ian before he continued. He asked if I could afford to walk away from everything and lose my investment, as that would be the easiest route to follow. I reasoned that although I could, however out of principle I wouldn't, because I had worked really hard for that money. I couldn't believe that the other things were so straightforward to solve though. I again thanked Ian for his time and help before I went on my way.

Goodbye Cruel World

May, 2008

The last few months had been difficult. I had listened, taken on board and acted on the advice that I'd been given by Ian and others. I had blocked the bank account and contacted Companies House. Unfortunately, I was unable to get myself removed from the official documentation without the authority of the Director of the company, John. I do have to give credit where credit is due, because I was promised every single penny back that I had invested into the business. However, after a few months of receiving minimal payments, I worked out that it would take John about ten years to pay me back what I was owed. I thought about the money and realised I was just being stubborn because of everything else that had happened. I had even kept my engagement ring as collateral, to ensure that John did pay me back (I never wanted to keep it). After four months or so, I decided I didn't want to stay in contact with John during the time it would take for our financial issues to be resolved. I decided that I would prefer to avoid contact of any kind, because I felt the current situation was preventing me from moving forward. Even if it meant losing my money, I needed a clean break.

Finally I built up the courage and penned John an email asking for him to meet me so that we could discuss things as 'adults' and hopefully come to some kind of agreement regarding our financial

168

affairs. My thinking was that if I could get a half decent lump sum, I would walk away and that would be the end of things. We arranged to meet in a local bar. I had the figure of just £1,000 in my head, which was much, much less than I had put in as an investment, but it would have been a token at least towards recognition of my contribution. I got myself a drink and sat down to discuss things. It was a very tense atmosphere, to say the least, but I had moved on from the anger and just wanted all ties cutting now, so that I could concentrate on getting myself well and getting on with the rest of my new life.

I asked John to start and I let him have his say with no interruptions. I was curious to know just what he would offer me. As I sat there listening intently to him, I couldn't believe that nearly three years of a relationship that had almost become a marriage had boiled down to this one moment! I totally agreed with John that because my sister Kelli had come to the USA and Mexico with me instead of him, this expense should be taken in to account and removed from any settlement figure, but the moment that he said he wanted a light switch (yes, you read that correctly!), a light switch that he had bought and put up in the house to be taken into consideration, I gave up any kind of hope of an adult discussion! I wanted to laugh at him because it really was so pathetic. But I didn't. Instead, I just fished inside my purse for the beautiful diamond engagement ring which had once taken pride of place on my left hand, and slid it across the table. I told him to keep his money (*my* money) and I walked away.

June, 6th, 2008

My 30th birthday was less than three months away. My life was so massively different from what I would have expected and imagined at the beginning of the year. I had finally made a huge change in my life and it was something that I had needed to do for a long, long time. I was only too aware that the other components of my path to self destruction now also needed to be addressed. I decided to write myself a letter addressing what needed to change and why. I sealed the letter within a birthday card, tying the envelope with pretty ribbons and a bow and secreting it underneath my mattress. The card was addressed to me, to be opened on 17th August. I had decided that the day I turned thirty was to be the day that I was going to take back control of my life.

Dear Jo,

I know you find it difficult to compliment yourself or take compliments from other people. You've spent the last eighteen years punishing yourself and forever trying to be over-perfect in a bid to get acceptance from and to please other people.

From today I want you to start living your life, not to please anyone but yourself. I want you to get the help that you need and to deal with all of your issues; but most of all it is time that you allowed yourself to be happy. No one is perfect, but you are you and you are perfect, just for you. No one else can ever be you, even if they tried to be, because you are unique and you are beautiful! Your constant need to be perfect makes you feel worse about

170

yourself. You need to accept what you are, and that is a good person and you are as good as the next. The more you try to improve yourself, the more imperfections you will find. Start loving yourself and start to see the good things in yourself that other people see in you. To achieve this happiness, you need to do the following:

- No more dieting
- No more purging and binging
- No more obsessing about body weight or shape
- No more self loathing
- No more cosmetic surgery
- No more binge drinking to run away from your problems
- No more allowing yourself to be walked all over
- No more worrying about what people think of you

and

- Let people who wrong you go
- Stop isolating yourself
- Refrain from obsessive worrying
- Stop feeling guilty about things you have no control over
- Stop being ashamed of who you are
- Stop being scared to be happy

Happy Birthday from the future, happier and healthier Jo xx

August, 2008

I had decided to wait until my birthday to implement my new life rules because I had already planned to do so much with friends for my birthday this year. I was going to have two celebrations (hey, if it's good enough for the Queen, then it's good enough for me!). One event involved a few friends from work who kidnapped me, bungled me on onto a train to Belgium, and force fed me thirty different types of Belgian beer over a two day period. I have NEVER, EVER, been so ill in my life! Nor had I ever before drunk out of a skull, been locked in a coffin or brought a karaoke bar to silence by singing so loudly out of key – all these things I managed to achieve in a very memorable 48 hours (does that sound a bit like one of the Hangover movies?!).

The second event I had planned was with my two closest friends, Emma and Becky, and my sister Kelli. I had wanted an intimate gathering at a French restaurant that I loved. I'd been offered champagne, the works, to mark my special occasion, but I opted for my favourite bottle of red wine because bubbles really don't agree with me. I had wanted this to be a quiet and tame evening because I had planned to tell my sister and my friends about the birthday gift I was going to give myself the following day. I knew the evening wasn't going to end as planned when I saw Kelli and Becky heading back from the bar with shots of Black Sambuca. Unfortunately, I remember very little about the evening after the first four shots (what can I say? I'm a lightweight!). Apparently, I was carried to bed by Becky, who took off my boots. I then threw my legs in the air, slurring "Jeans,

172

jeans!" As Becky went to pull my jeans off for me, she struggled and actually pulled me half-way down the hallway! Oh well, when at last, my life flashes before my eyes, I will laugh and can say I really had some fun along the way, even if I can't remember most of it!

The following day, I waited until everyone else had gone home before I opened my gift to myself, reading the letter for the first time in over two months. Finally, I was ready for this monumental battle; I had partied far too hard for far too long and I had damaged myself in so many ways along the way. I was now strong enough to face this fight full on. Most importantly, I really wanted to do it.

I walked into the bedroom and headed straight to my underwear drawer, opening it and lifting out the baskets. Hidden for almost three and a half years, beneath these baskets, where I knew no one would look, were the leaflets that Darren had given to me. (Thank you Darren. I know how desperate you were to help me. I'm not sure you understood at the time that I could only help myself when the time was right, but now that time had finally come, and thanks to you I had the information I needed!). I made myself a cup of tea and sat down to read the information about the CARALINE centre for eating disorders. I read the leaflets from front to back for the first time. I did shed tears, but they were not tears of sadness, they were tears of happiness because I knew I really could do it! I had taken the first step, I had admitted to myself, for the first time, that I did have a problem. Now, I wanted to deal with it head on. No matter what, I would do this.

I grabbed the phone and carefully punched in the helpline number. As it began to ring, I started to shake, and then . . .

"Good afternoon, you are through to the Caraline helpline, how can I help you?"

. . . I took a deep breath . . .

"Hello, my name is Jo and I need your help."

"Hi Jo, my name is Emily. What is it that I can help you with today?"

"Hi Emily, I have an eating disorder but I no longer want it to be part of my life, I want to be well and I want to be happy."

(Just saying that out loud for the first time felt so bloody good!)

"That's something I can definitely help you with, but to do that I need to ask you some questions, to work out the most appropriate help for you. Are you happy to answer these questions?"

. . . another deep breath . . .

"I'm happy to answer your questions."

"OK, Jo, I need you to be honest with me, if you feel you need to stop then just let me know. This conversation is about *you* and helping you to get the help that you need; I am not here to catch you out or make you do or say anything you don't want to, do you understand?"

"Yes, I understand."

"OK, I need to make some notes as we are talking. Are you ready?"

I had no idea what I was going to be asked, I was anxious and I was scared, but I knew that I had to be totally honest with Emily if I was going to get myself well again.

I spent approximately an hour of my 30th birthday speaking to Emily on the telephone, as she listened and took notes about some of my most private of thoughts. I had never before shared with anyone so many of the facts. Of course there were people who knew snippets, and what I wanted them to know, but Emily, who I had never even met, was now learning things about me that no one else knew. At the end of the question and answer session, I was told that I was a suitable candidate to receive treatment, and was invited to a group session at Kiln House in Luton. As I arrived, I almost turned my car around, because I didn't know what to expect and was frightened. I was now way, way out of my comfort zone. Instead, I forced myself to get out of the car. I had come too far forward to step backwards yet again.

August 26th, 2008

I found myself in a room with one man and eight women, two of whom worked for Caraline. That left eight of us who had bulimia or anorexia (or a combination of the two, anorexia binge purge subtype). Each person was asked to introduce themselves to the rest of the group. We were told to say our names, but reassured that anything else that we chose to share was done so on a voluntary basis. No one would be made to speak if they preferred not to. This made me relax a little, because now the pressure had been removed: I could say as much or as little as I wished.

It was also explained that anything that was said in this room was private and shouldn't be disclosed outside these four walls. The two Caraline women introduced themselves as Megan and Emily and it made me feel even more at ease being able to put a face to the name of the person I'd spoken to the week before. As the session got underway, and I listened to the other participants telling their stories, I realised that this group probably wasn't the right thing for me at this time. Although I could see similarities with the others, some of them didn't seem to genuinely want to get well. Some had been made to get help and had been sent to Caraline (like when Darren had tried to make me), while others were doing the group therapy for other people. I would have fitted into the group perfectly a few months ago, but having made the decision to get well, and knowing that I was finally doing this for me and for me alone, I felt rather uncomfortable. As it got to my turn, I introduced myself and told the group that I had bulimia and that I had had it for almost 18 years. The only other thing I said was that this was my first time at an eating disorders therapy session. Emily stood up and congratulated me on taking this huge step forward and everyone clapped me for making this move on my road to recovery, but it all felt so false.

I approached Emily after the session and explained how I felt, telling her that group therapy wasn't the right thing for me, and that I wouldn't be returning. Please understand that I'm not saying that group therapy is a bad thing. I know it works really well for some people. But I was used to doing things on my own. I was a very private person until I started writing this book! I knew I needed help, that this wasn't something I could do alone, but I also knew that bearing my soul to a group of strangers didn't feel safe or comfortable. To some degree, my group therapy had been the pro-anorexia websites. I knew there were other people out there with similar problems to my own, but it wasn't their support I needed at this stage in my own journey. I guess this book is also a bit of group therapy, because now I am ready to talk to more people about what I've been through and how I've come out the other side, and if I can help just one person to help themselves through being so open, then my hopes will have been realised.

Emily was very understanding, and gave me the details of two private therapists that she knew who she thought might be able to help me to overcome my eating problems. The following day, I called one of them and made an appointment to see her the following week.

September 3rd, 2008

I arrived at the therapist's office a little early and was checked in and offered a drink. I picked up a magazine, as I settled down for a short wait. As I looked down, reading, there was a tap on my shoulder. I looked up to see a work colleague standing in front of me. "Hi Jo, fancy seeing you here." I couldn't believe it, and forced a smile back "Hi Phil, how are you?" He told me he was fine and then asked me what I was doing there! I might have had lots I needed to change, but I thanked God for my quick thinking and prayed this was a skill I'd never lose. "Oh, I'm just here as moral support for a friend. You?" "Me? I'm picking the Mrs up." he explained, nodding towards the receptionist! My mind was racing, and I was suddenly beginning to feel sick and dizzy, thinking that I had been sprung. The idea of being seen in a therapist's office by someone I knew terrified me. My phone started to ring in my bag, so fumbled around and grabbed it before apologising to Phil. I stood up and told the receptionist that I really needed to take this call and I'd be back in just a few minutes. Of course, that wasn't true. I cancelled the call as soon as I was the other side of the door, ran to my car and drove home in pieces. I was convinced that by the time I got in to work the following day everyone would be talking about me and sniggering behind my back (very little stays secret on the prison service grapevine).

Driving home, my mind was on overdrive. I had a thousand things racing around it, like what would I say if Phil did tell someone and it got out. That one thought alone terrified me so much that I had to pull my car over and throw up; I'd wound myself up so much worrying. As I got back into the car, I felt an overwhelming need to binge like I had never before - it was in this moment I truly realised my fears of not being accepted and of what people thought of me. My eating, my self-loathing, my depression and everything else, boiled down to something much larger - my need to be in CONTROL. I was a control freak! While it was easy to sit and blame other people, the reality was that all these problems of mine were created by no one but myself. I had made my own choices in life. My eating was just a small part of the problem; I now realised I was battling something much, much, bigger.

My urge to binge was so all consuming that I had to go the supermarket for food before going home. I knew that I had made major progress in my life. I had taken those two steps towards getting help and I knew this would push me three steps backwards, but I *had* to satisfy Annie because she was the only thing in my life that I felt truly in control of. Walking up and down the aisles, picking up chocolates, biscuits, crisps, sausage rolls, ice-cream and all the other bad and banned foods from my list, I felt so good knowing how it would make me feel, in just a little while. The warm satisfying feeling that pulsated through my veins as I ate and I ate. If anyone ever saw me during a binge, I doubt that they would ever be able to look at me the same way again. But at the time I didn't care, because once I was finished I knew that Annie would then talk to me in her soothing manner, "See how much better you feel?" And it would make me feel so good for at least a little while.

Then I looked down at my bulging basket again, which was actually hurting my arm to the point of leaving red welts because it was so full. Suddenly, I felt disgusted. This was a new feeling, something I had not yet experienced in regards to Annie - pure repulsion. Sure, I hated myself for doing what I did to myself, but this was something much stronger than that. I spun around and back tracked, placing all the items in my basket back on the shelves. Now I was now battling myself in the middle of a supermarket! Annie wanted this binge more than anything, but I didn't want to give in to it, I wanted to fight against her, and I really believed I could do it. I hadn't binged for five days, which was a major achievement for me. I didn't want to be defeated now. I took a deep breath, and composed myself before I began to do my 'standard' shop, fighting to ignore the urge to pick up binge foods. Then I got to the chocolate aisle, and picked up a family size galaxy bar. I put it into my basket and then put it back on the shelf again; then back in to my basket and then back on the shelf again. As I continued doing this, I realised that this was my own personal war I was fighting.

A man I had never met before approached me "Hey, you know you've been wrestling with that chocolate bar for the past five minutes, don't you?" I looked up at him and flashed my sweet shallow smile before saying "Oh you know what us women are like; I have a holiday coming up and need to look good on the beach." I was laughing as I talked to him, but inside I was wondering what he must think of me, did I look really nuts? He gave me a little nudge and a cheeky wink before telling me that a little bit of what I fancied wouldn't hurt.

I smiled again, before putting the chocolate back on the shelf, saying "No, I best not, I best be good," before walking away to carry on with the rest of my shopping. I was just about to finish my shopping, when I ended up back down the chocolate aisle and I bumped in to him again! "Are you still fighting with that bar of chocolate?" he asked. I laughed and asked him if he was my Supermarket Stalker. We both laughed and I headed off to the checkout.

When I got home, I was so proud of myself for having walked away from this binge, this fight had been won. I began to unpack my bags in the kitchen and was surprised when I came across a galaxy chocolate bar tucked inside one of them with a post-it note stuck on the top, saying "Enjoy. From your Supermarket Stalker," with a phone number which I assume was his! Now this would have been very funny, had it not been for the fact that I had fought so hard to resist the urge to buy it! You guessed it - I ended up breaking and gave in to my deepest darkest desire. I began raiding the cupboards to any find stodgy food I could to satisfy myself. A kilogram bag of pasta which I threw in to pans of water; four tins of tuna and a bottle of mayonnaise; three tins of sweetcorn. While the pasta was cooking, I ate three sausage rolls from the fridge and then grabbed a box of cereal and ate two huge bowls chewing each mouthful religiously thirty times, before swallowing, and then washing it down with a gulp of water.

These binging rituals had logic as a base. With something sharp and dry like cereal, if I chewed and chewed and followed each bite with some liquid then the whole mess would be much softer and less painful on the way back up. I also used a teaspoon because I felt less greedy if I was taking smaller mouthfuls.

When the pasta was ready, I mixed all the ingredients together in to a huge salad bowl and consumed the lot before eating the bar of chocolate.

MYSELF, ME AND I

In that one sitting alone, I had consumed over eleven thousand calories. Nobody can eat like a bulimic can, it's like you're an animal on a feeding frenzy, it really grotesque deed at hand. When I was binging; I felt like I was taken hostage by Annie and my own body and there was absolutely nothing I could do to stop it.

It took me well over an hour to complete this binge. This was by far my biggest, worst binge ever. As I finished the last mouthful, I was, as always, consumed with an overwhelming sense of guilt and greed that now made me really feel like utter crap.

I ran into the bathroom as fast as I could and tied my hair tightly back into a pony tail, so that it wouldn't be in my face. Then I forced my fingers down my throat time and time again. This was by far worse than any other time I could ever remember. Because the binge had been so large, I just had to keep going and going. I *needed* to get this food out of my body. Then suddenly I began choking and I couldn't breathe; something had become trapped in my throat and I couldn't dislodge it. I pushed my fingers even further down my throat to try and move it. I tried coughing and slapping my chest to shift it, but nothing. It was only then I started to panic. Now I was getting really scared. I made a fist and started hammering on my own breast-bone really hard. Luckily, on the third attempt, this worked. But now the vomit was coming out of both my mouth and my nose and missing the toilet basin. It covered the walls and floor as it exited my body like some kind of arterial spray.

Sugar Coating

When my purge had finished, I sat back on the floor, gasping for breath. Once I had managed to regain control of my breathing, I began to scream for the longest of times. I screamed so loud. I screamed for all the hurt I was feeling, for all the anger that was inside me, for all the loneliness and for all the pain and fear that I had felt over the years, for all the jealousy of seeing others happy in their lives when mine was so miserable, for all self loathing that I felt, for all the times I had done this to myself and allowed myself to be hurt by others, and finally for all the times I had pushed my feelings deep inside and hidden them away, thinking that I could cope all on my own, when in fact I had just piled new issues on top of the old issues. Now, I was erupting, like a volcano spilling its lava out of its highest peak, after years of allowing the pressure to build up inside its deepest of chambers.

But now I wanted someone to hear me. Now, I wanted someone to come and help me. Now, I wanted someone to come and save me. But no one heard me, and no one came. So I just curled up on the floor like a child in the foetal position inside a mother's womb, because I wanted to feel safe and warm again, I no longer wanted to feel this sad or this alone. In those moments that I couldn't breathe, I really had thought that this was how I was going to die. Not being able breathe had been the scariest thing that had ever happened to me. In those few moments, I had imagined myself dying in a puddle of my own vomit, with no one to help me or save me. I hadn't wanted anyone to find me like that - having that lasting memory of me implanted inside their brain forever! I was now aware just how out of control I really had become. This binge purge had *really* frightened me.

I finally found the energy to clean the bathroom and then myself up, before I went back in to the lounge, which was where I often did my deep thinking and my diary writing. On this day I wrote to all the Myselfs, all the Annie's, in the world:

So you want to be bulimic, huh? Bulimia, I know, is not supposed to be an accepted form of weight loss. Yet I constantly read stories of girls begging for tips on how to make their purges easier. Let me tell you something, bulimia is not meant to be a walk in the park, it is not meant to provide you with a healthy lifestyle. But you still insist on 'learning the tips and tricks of the trade'. If you still really want an eating disorder, then the only thing that you are blessed with is ignorance and a very long, lonely, and sad existence.

But I was already bulimic, I had been exercising for years, I had been taking laxatives for years, I had been . . . blah, blah, blah. Have you? I don't believe you. If indeed you have, then just continue on with what you're doing, because believe me, that is already bad enough! You don't need me to metaphorically stick my fingers down your throat for you. But you girls still log on to these websites and you still keep asking. So . . . here goes . . . I will tell you everything that you want to know, with no holding back, if you're sure that's what you want!

Allow me to describe the path that you're heading down, the path that I know so very well. It's a path I've had to fight with my very life to leave. Allow me to describe the damage I have done to myself by choosing this path.

Firstly, you will have to become a pig. A fat, greedy, worthless and selfish pig. A pig that will eat everything that's in sight and yet will still come back for more, and even more. A pig who will steal food, even from their family and friends, because you simply can't say no to that chocolate bar. A pig who goes to the shops to buy litres of ice cream, bags of crisps, bars of chocolate, packs of biscuits and then eats them all in one sitting. A pig that will eat right out of the packets while getting food all over your face and down the front of your clothes! The ice cream is so cold but you will still use your hands to shovel it into your mouth, because you've got to get it inside you. You have to stop thinking when you binge, because the food takes over. Some of us think that this is a good thing! But remember that we are just greedy pigs. Maybe you will adapt and start using a tea spoon, like I did, so that you can justify to yourself that you aren't being that greedy! Maybe you'll start to blend your food, throwing it all in a food processor and drinking it through a straw. Whatever you decided to do, you will find a way to justify it to yourself . . .

Secondly, you will start to hate yourself! You'll hate yourself for what you've just done. You will have to hate yourself for what you did yesterday and you'll hate yourself for what you know you'll do tomorrow. You have to hate yourself because food has total control over you! You can fight to regain control, but it is a hard fight and you have to really, really want it (and believe that you can do it).

Then you will move to step three - you will have to purge. You will have to purge to get rid of the food and you will have to purge so that you can regain the illusion of control. You will need to get rid of the food-poison that you've just put inside your body. You have to get everything out of you, because if you don't, then the food has won, because it's got the better of you. God forbid, if you have issues with being fat. Don't worry, most of us do. Maybe you'll decide to take laxatives too. You'll start off small, two or three perhaps, but then you'll have to double the dose, and then triple it. The next thing you know you will be out of control with this as well, and suddenly you're taking up to sixty a day. You'll have so much stomach pain and cramps that they will wake you up during the night, you will be in so much pain that you can't move and so you don't make it to the bathroom; you didn't make it to the bathroom and there is shit all over you and all over your bedding! You are an adult, and yet you didn't make it to the toilet. You will hate yourself a little bit more, while cleaning yourself up and hiding the evidence from those around you. Because you don't want them to know what has just happened. So you'll pretend instead that you started your period or something. I hate to be crude, but I'm being realistic, I would be lying to you if I sugar coated anything...

Maybe you'll decide to exercise. Now if you do this you're on a very fast road to anorexia. You will exercise all the time, day and night. You'll go to the gym three or four hours a day and you'll start to watch yourself lose weight. But then, you'll get carried away. You will be able to eat a chocolate bar and know exactly how far you'll have to run to get rid of the calories. (23 minutes at 6.5 miles per hour for a chocolate orange containing 210 calories and 12 grams of fat). You will look at your body and won't think that you're getting anywhere. Instead you'll think that you keep getting fatter and fatter every day. So, you will then start weighing yourself constantly, just to see whether you've lost a pound or not. Well done! You will have now become completely consumed with your body weight and body image. That you're boarding between bulimia and anorexia, with a little body dysmorphia added into the mix.

Perhaps you'll decide to puke, this is usually a bulimic's favourite when all else fails; there are always the trusted fingers, right? You'll go to the toilet, where you will have to fight against yourself. Sometimes you'll be on the verge of tears, because you're fighting that day and you don't want to puke. At other times, you'll no longer care. When things get really bad, you'll find that you're puking in an attempt to deal with all your other problems as well, not just the binging! You'll have to puke to get the poison out - the poison of everyday living, what your dad said to you as a child, because no one understands you, because you were bullied at school, because of your exam grades, because your best friend killed herself, because a boyfriend has raped you or because your boss at work is being a total bitch. But wait, don't think that puking has to be a reaction to a really, really bad day . . . puking will become the answer to even your most pathetic bad hair day. You'll eat because everything in your life sucks, and then you will puke to get rid of the food, the guilt, the crap in your life. In reality, by now you're making yourself puke to mask your problems. Sometimes things will get so bad that you can't even eat, but you'll still have to puke to get the poison of your life out from inside of you.

You'll go to the toilet where you'll have to shove your fingers so far down your throat it hurts. You will get puke in your hair if you're not careful, and all over your face, but you'll no longer care, and will just continue to puke and puke, until you're puking nothing but an orangey bile which tastes like poison. You won't be able to stop, because there'll be an underlying fear that you've failed again and that you didn't get everything out – yes, that's right, you failed if you left something inside! So you'll keep puking even though the toilet is full, and you can see that everything's out. Then you'll start analysing your puke to make sure that you did, in fact, get it all out! You will have taken mental notes of what you were binging so you can monitor if it has come back up or not. Depending on how soon after your binge, it will also taste just the same coming out the opposite direction as it did when it was ingested.

But let's not forget that you've have just been eating ice cream with those same fingers that you're now puking with so that you can make more room . . . so that you can continue to binge. You'll not stop to wash your hands, because you no longer care! You'll put them back in your mouth, with pieces of vomit

188

and food all over them and repeat the regime above. But wait a minute, because you've not quite finished just yet - the cravings still won't have gone. So you'll go to the drive through, or the supermarket, or the shops, or to a restaurant - wherever you'll be able to get more food. But first you'll have go to the bank. Let us not forget about the bank, because you will spend ALL of your spare money on food, laxatives, water pills and diet pills, because you won't be able to say no.

Prepare yourself for embarrassment and humiliation, especially when your friends and family find out. You'll know that they know exactly what you're doing when you leave the house to go to the shop. They'll know that you've already been to the supermarket twice today, buying baskets full of junk food each time. Or are you getting paranoid now too, adding that into your list of issues? This is why you'll try to keep it secret and lie to everyone. That's right, you'll have to become a liar, you'll have to become deceitful, and you'll have become clever and cunning, because you'll see the situation as choice less. Then you will reach a new low. You'll fetch the food you threw away earlier from out of the bin, because you'll have nothing left in the house to eat and you'll NEED to eat. You had thrown the food away so that you wouldn't eat it, but now you'll be living like a tramp and eating it from the bin.

Lastly, you'll have to deal with the side effects, if walking around smelling like puke and shit while eating like a pig isn't bad enough for you! Or the guy at the checkout that will look at you strangely, because this is your third visit in one day. How about the fact that you'll struggle to maintain relationships and friendships, and to live like everyone else does. But that's just for starters . . . you're just going love the rest of the side effects! You've always loved your long blonde hair, haven't you? It's thick and healthy and has always been one of your best features. Everyone has commented on it: "I wish I had hair like yours, Jo," they've said. (Do insert your own name and hair colour/style as appropriate!) But now it's falling out. You'll shower and find that it's coming out in clumps when you wash it. You'll notice that it's all over the walls when you brush it. So you'll cut it all off short, so you can on keep binging and purging . . . Then your body will start to act in a strange way. Your periods will stop or at least become irregular, your heart will beat irregularly and your stomach will be bloated. You'll have heart burn all the time and end up living on Gaviscon. Your teeth will hurt and will bleed when you brush them. You'll feel faint, and will sometimes actually faint, when you stand up for too long. Your skin will be dry and blotchy. Your throat will be constantly sore from forcing your fingers down it. Your fingers will be cut and your knuckles will be ripped from scraping against your teeth as you've pushed them down into your throat time and time again! You'll no longer be able to go to the toilet unless you're taking laxatives, and you'll worry that you thought you saw blood the last time you threw up! You'll look terrible. But by this time, there is no way out.

There isn't any way out except for death. You'll be killing yourself for a sausage roll (or whatever is your binge favourite) and you'll get to a point where you no longer care. You'll be killing yourself for that

190

sausage roll, and puking it up is simply a part of eating it in the first place. Perhaps you'll quit. I did that . . . all the time. Don't forget, I had had my face in the toilet less than an hour before I sat and wrote this diary entry for you. But, I've promised myself that that was truly the last time. Quitting so fast, because it really is that easy. Then those sausage rolls you threw away will start calling to you, and you'll wish they would just Shut The Fuck Up! "Let it happen . . . go . . . go eat your heart out!" Your own Annie will be saying to you!

So, I've now provided you with all the information you could ever need to become a successful bulimic! You know exactly how you'll feel, how you'll have to think and everything that is expected of you. What you do now is up to you.

What I did then was up to me. I wanted to stop. I really did. I didn't yet know how, but I knew I was going to beat Annie. I was determined to win this fight or I would die trying!

So I got out the Yellow Pages and began my search for more therapists in Milton Keynes. All I knew was that I wanted someone who worked from home, because I couldn't risk the same situation as before, when Phil had spotted me. I also believed I wanted a female therapist because I was sure a woman would understand me more. I also had so many trust issues with men that I felt I wouldn't be able to open up like I would to another woman. I found a therapist called Stacey and booked my first appointment to see her.

October 9th, 2008

I arrived just after 6pm. I had had to schedule my appointments around my shift pattern because I didn't want anyone at work to know (apart from the very few friends who already did of course). I was particularly concerned about anyone knowing because one of the questions on my application form, back in 2003, had been "Have you ever suffered from an eating disorder?" Of course at the time I had lied, so I was now concerned that if my problems did come to light I would get in trouble and could even lose my job. Well, I say I lied, but that's not strictly true. I had still been in denial about my eating problems and I hadn't, at that stage, even admitted the problem to myself. It had never affected my work during my time in the Prison Service apart from the one time that I was late on duty. I had never taken time off sick because of my eating problems. However, it is classed as a mental illness. I figured it could go either way, either I would get in trouble or they would support me, but being the pessimistic person that I was, I decided that I wasn't going to take the risk of finding out which.

Stacey took me through to her office, where she explained to me how she worked as a therapist, so I knew exactly what to expect from her. She asked me about myself and what had brought me to see her. I'm not sure why, but I didn't feel comfortable with her very direct approach. I went to see her a few more times, but most of my sessions involved me sitting there in silence. I don't want to say I didn't like Stacey, because I didn't know her, but if I was unable to be open with her then there was no point in me wasting my time or money being in these sessions. So by the end of November I decided not to return, and once again I set about looking for a therapist.

December, 2008

So here I was, back to square one again and still convinced I wanted a female therapist. But then I came across Stuart's advert and for some reason felt drawn towards his number. So I picked up the phone and called him, just before Christmas. Because of the holidays, I wasn't able to get an appointment until the third week of January, but after a few minutes on the phone with Stuart, I was more than happy to wait, hoping that I might, at last, have found the right therapist.

January 23rd, 2009

18 years, 7 months and 6 days after my first ever binge, after 18 years, 7 months and 6 days of self loathing and self inflicted torture, after spending 18 years, 7 months and 6 days of going nowhere. Wasting 18 years, 7 months and 6 days destroying any ounce of my self esteem, when I should have been having the best years of my life; I arrived at Stuart's little cottage in Stony Stratford where I was met by a gentleman that I would describe as a 'hippy'. His long grey hair was tied back in a ponytail and he wasn't at all what I was expecting, but he made me feel very comfortable. I went in to his house and I was taken through to his 'work area', as

he called it. This was just a back room that he'd made in to a workable space. I liked it because it was homely, not at all like the other clinical places I had been to before. Stuart offered me a drink and I asked for a cup of tea. He returned with a cup of camomile tea, which he described as very calming as he handed it to me.

I took a sip because I didn't want to appear rude, but I didn't like it and wished he'd brought me a normal cup of tea instead! Stuart saw me wince and looked at me over the top of his glasses "Persevere with it, it gets better." I wasn't convinced, but I continued to drink it, and of course he was right. Stuart sat behind his desk, pulled out some paper, and explained that he needed to get some details from me. He started with "What is your full name?" "Joanne-Lynn Allott, but I prefer to be called Jo." "OK, JoJo, what can I do for you?" This made me laugh and put me instantly at ease, because no one had ever called me JoJo except for Jennie, and no one knew that but the two of us. It was at this moment I knew for sure that Stuart was the therapist for me.

Stuart wrote down all my basic information, such as my date of birth etc and then put his pen down, took off his glasses and asked "So, JoJo, what can I help you with? Why have you come to see me?" I didn't even have to think about my answer, I just blurted it out. "I have bulimia, among other things, and I really need some help." Stuart gave me a gentle, fatherly smile, before saying "Well done, Honey, that's the hardest bit out of the way. Now tell me, why do you do it?" "There are so many reasons I don't know where to start." Stuart just smiled again "How about at the beginning. That's normally a good place I find." So I did. I went right back to the beginning.

"I was bullied for being fat and ugly, even by my own dad, who wanted to pay me a pound in money for every pound in weight I lost, when I was just twelve years old. It started off as a diet, for me to lose weight, then that turned into me trying not to eat and starving myself for days. Then, when I was so hungry I would eat whatever I could find. I would then make myself sick so I wouldn't get any fatter, because I didn't want to disappoint my dad." As I sat, talking and talking, I let all my hurt and anger go. I felt comfortable and happy that I was finally saying everything aloud. All the time I had been seeing Stacey, I never told her any of this stuff, and yet here I was, telling Stuart *everything* within minutes. For the rest of my hour, I didn't stop talking. As the hour drew closer to an end, I kept looking at my watch. Stuart noticed, and insisted that I take off my watch and give it to him. He extended his hand across the desk, and I did as I was told, before asking why he wanted it. Again, he smiled, "I don't work by the hour, even though my rates are hourly. Every person is different and time is irrelevant in here. You obviously haven't finished, and I don't want to stop you until you're ready. Luckily, you're my only client today." I couldn't believe what I was hearing. He was so different to what I was expecting from a therapist. I spent over two and a half hours with Stuart on this first visit. The opportunity to let everything go, to get all my hurt out in the open, and to be totally honest with someone for the first time ever in my life was fantastic, but also exhausting. As my story ended, I asked Stuart what I owed him. "Just £25 please Honey." I looked at him quizzically, "Stuart, don't be so ridiculous! I've had two and a half times that. Please." "JoJo, I just want to help you to help yourself. I told you, time isn't important; but helping you is." I couldn't believe I found such a beautiful soul, someone who genuinely wanted to help me!

Stuart spoke again "Oh, there is one final thing that I want you to start doing before you come and see me next, and I want you to do this every single day until you believe it!" With some trepidation, I asked him what he wanted me to do. "Every time you look in a mirror or shop window, I want you to say to yourself "I am a beautiful woman and I am good enough. I am beautiful inside and I am beautiful on the outside. You need to say this every day until it sinks in and you believe it. Do you understand me?" I smiled, "But I can't say it if people are around me. How crazy do you think I really am?" Stuart laughed, "JoJo, you are not crazy, and if people are around, then on those occasions you say it silently to yourself. It's doing it that's important. Do you understand me?" I said I did and I would, but to be honest I wasn't being honest, I didn't think for one minute that I would actually say or do it. I got home later that night and I thought about my session with Stuart at great length. I reminded myself why I was doing this, and of the promise I'd made to myself to do *whatever I had to do*, to get myself well again.

If saying this phrase to myself in the mirror daily was to be part of my recovery, then I would do it, particularly as I liked Stuart. I stood up and walked in to my bedroom, where I undressed, and looked at myself properly, naked. I muttered the phrase for the very first time. *I am a beautiful woman. I am good enough. I am beautiful on the inside as well as the out. I am a beautiful woman. I am good enough. I am beautiful on the inside as well as the out.*

Coming Back to Life

The following week, I visited Stuart again and willingly drank my camomile tea. He started the session by asking me if I had begun working on myself in front of the mirror and I reassured him I had. We then spoke about how this was making me feel. Towards the end of the session, Stuart went in to his top drawer and slid a book across the table to me. Without saying a word, I picked up the book and read the title. Stuart explained that he had been in Glastonbury that weekend and had stumbled across the book at a market. He thought it would be worth me reading it before he and I went any further. I read the title again, this time aloud: "Overcoming Perfectionism." I was puzzled and told Stuart I didn't understand. What was it all about? What did it have to do with me? I'd never heard the word Perfectionism before. Stuart reassured me that it would all make sense when I started to read it, and asked me if I trusted him. I thought about this, and was surprised to realise that although I didn't know him well, I really did trust him. Otherwise, how could I have felt so comfortable talking to him in such detail? "Then Honey," he replied, smiling, "I think we can sort you out!" Our session ended and I paid for the hour and for the book. I got out my diary and asked Stuart when I could book in my next appointment. "When you've read the book and not before," he replied. I didn't understand the relevance of this, or its meaning, but I wouldn't see Stuart again for another two months. When I got home, I immediately pulled the book out of my bag and started to read it. By page eleven, I felt as though it had been written about me! It explained me so well. I did the first self-help task, to find out whether or not I did have 'Perfectionism'.

Common negative effects of Perfectionism:

Emotional (feelings)

- Anxiety (e.g. feeling nervous, stressed)
- Depression (e.g. feeling sad, low in mood)

Social

- Social isolation
- Narrow interests
- Focusing almost all of one's time on a particular area (e.g. focusing mainly on work and rarely socialising)
- Limiting pleasurable activities not seen as being related to achievement (e.g. never just reading a magazine or listening to music)

Physical

- Insomnia
- Exhaustion and tiredness
- Muscle tension
- Upset Stomach

Cognitive (thinking)

- Poor concentration
- Rumination (e.g. thinking about a mistake made in a task over and over again)

- Increased self-criticism
- Low self-esteem

Behavioural

- Repeated checking (e.g. reading an email over and over again before sending it, to check the text is completely accurate)
- Repeating tasks (e.g. rewriting and editing something over and over)
- Excessive amount of time on tasks (e.g. taking six hours to clean your kitchen)
- Avoiding tasks
- Putting off tasks (procrastination)
- List-making
- Being over thorough
- Hating to waste time and, as a consequence, being over busy!

Each of these things I did. Every single one, apart from having poor concentration or socially isolating myself. How sad is that? Being a perfectionist is not, in itself, a bad thing, but when it becomes negative perfectionism, like mine had, combined with all my other issues, then it can be very damaging. I decided that the first thing I needed to do was to write myself a Bucket List of all the things that I wanted to accomplish in my new life.

1. Tackle my eating disorder, drinking and other issues.

2. Allow myself to be happy and healthy. Then when body confident with myself, go and do a Gok Wang - have a boudoir photo shoot.

3. Jump out of an aeroplane (which I had wanted to do for so long).

4. Appear on television.

5. Study and get some qualifications behind me.

6. Do well at work.

7. Learn to speak Spanish.

8. Trek the Machu Picchu for charity.

9. Watch the sun rise over Ayres Rock, Uluru.

10. Learn to play the saxophone.

February, 2009

I knew I had to finish the book before I saw Stuart again, but I also started to make some changes in my life.

I was successful in getting a promotion at work. Although it was only a temporary position, I was delighted with my achievement. The year before, I had almost burst into tears during the interview and my feedback had been, that I was nervous wreck that looked like a startled rabbit in front of car headlights as it was about to be hit! This time, I was so much more confident in myself and the answers that I'd given.

I applied to appear on a game show! This started off as a joke at work when some of the men on the unit I was working on at the time were watching Golden Balls, hosted by Jasper Carrot. For anyone who hasn't seen the programme, it's a game about convincing others that you have all the money, even if you haven't; there is no skill involved, apart from your ability to persuade others. As the show was coming to an end, one of the prisoners turned to me and said "Here Jo, you should go on that because we never know when you're telling the truth!" I wasn't sure whether I was offended by that and said as much, but his response was to explain that he only meant that I was good at Poker, and that it was impossible to tell whether I had a good hand or not. I laughed, and as the credits to the show came up, they actually said that they were looking for new contestants! These coincidences keep happening in my life, don't they?

When I got home later that evening, I switched on my computer and decided I would apply for the show. After all, an appearance on TV was one of the goals on my Bucket List. I didn't think that I would get anywhere, but what did I have to lose? A few days later I received a call from the producers working at ITV inviting me to attend an audition which was being held in Nottingham on the 12th of February. I grabbed my work diary and looked at my shift pattern. I was on a late shift that day, so despite the short notice, I could go! I decided that I would go up the evening before and see my mum, killing two birds with one stone. I was advised to prepare a speech about myself lasting a couple of minutes, but I didn't bother, deciding I would just turn up and wing it, as I wasn't expecting to actually get through anyway.

The following morning, I arrived at the Hilton hotel in Nottingham at about 8am, and was ushered into a room with fifteen other people who had also applied to be on the show. We were each shown to our seats, which were arranged in a horseshoe shape. With two members of the production crew watching us, the guy at the side of me was told to stand up first and tell us little about himself. This meant I would be last. One by one, as the other people did their spiel, I sat and listened to them, not yet knowing what I was going to say about myself. They were all so very prepared and had clearly had been practising. When finally it was my turn, I stood slowly and from nowhere the first thing out of my mouth was "Hi! I'm Jo; Well I see you've saved the best till last!" I then bowed to the rest of the group and continued rambling on. I don't remember exactly what else I said but the whole room was in fits of laughter.

We were then split into two groups for the second part of the audition, where we had to take part in a 'fun debate'. With one team 'for' and one 'against', the rules were simple - you weren't allowed to interrupt anyone who was speaking; if you wanted to challenge someone's opinion, you had to raise your hand and stand up and you could have your say once they'd finished their point. I really bounced off a police officer, Lisa, who was in the other team, and everything she said I seemed to challenge and turn around so that my opinion was the better choice. One of the debate subjects was about vegetarians.

MYSELF, ME AND I

Lisa's team was against vegetarians and my team was in favour of vegetarians. Lisa raised her hand in the air and stood up, proclaiming "Vegetarian people are all malnourished and look anorexic!" As quick as a flash, my hand shot up in to the air and I stood up. As she finished, I turned to the right, which meant that the back of my body was now facing the camera. I bent forward, cheekily pointing at my ass, and asked "Does that look like the ass of an anorexic?" I sat back down without another word, but the room had again burst into fits of laughter. I really didn't understand how I'd said that, given that I *was* actually battling an eating disorder myself and was massively paranoid about the size of my own rear. Where this new-found confidence and ability to laugh at myself was coming from, I had no idea.

Once we finished this debating round, we were sent to get a drink and a snack while they made their decisions. I never dreamed for one minute I would get through, but I was genuinely pleased with myself for having had the confidence to get this far. After what seemed like a very long ten minutes, the two producers appeared and read out my name along with two others. I thought they were sending us home, but in fact we were the only ones who had got through to the next round. The three of us were taken back through to the audition room, where this time we had to test our skills of thinking on our feet by playing a mock up of the Golden Balls game. At the end of this, I was asked to attend the BBC studios in London the following week. I couldn't believe my luck! It was a rest day the following Friday, so I was off work. I was due to go travelling for six weeks the day after, so I thought why not give it a shot as I'd come this far. If nothing else, it would be a new experience.

The following week, I got an early train to Sheppard's Bush, arriving at the BBC studios shortly before 9am. I gave my name and invitation letter to the receptionist who made a call and then told me to go and sit down and that someone would come to collect me. I was there for about ten minutes when a good looking man approached me and introduced himself as Dean. He was to be my producer for the day. He took me to my dressing room, which I would be sharing with another woman called Joan. Dean explained what would happen and that the preliminary filming of captions that would later be inserted into the show would start at about 2pm. Before that, I would meet Jasper Carrot and go through some props to make sure I was camera ready. It all felt like such a blur and as if it wasn't really happening to me.

Here is a brief overview of the game, for those of you who haven't seen the show:

Round 1

The Golden Bank (a bit like a giant lottery machine) releases twelve golden balls, each valued with a cash amount anywhere from £10 to £75,000. Four 'killer' balls are added into the mix, and each of the four contestants receives four balls. They place two balls on their 'front row', visible to the other contestants, and two balls on their back row, visible only to themselves. They then announce, truthfully or not, the value of the balls on their back row. The contestants discuss who they think is lying and secretly vote for the person they think should leave the game (the person they believe has the lowest value in their four balls or the most killer balls). At the end of the round, the value of the back row balls is revealed, and the balls belonging to the person who has been voted off are removed from the game.

Round 2

The twelve remaining balls, two more cash balls and one killer ball are added and the fifteen balls are randomly divided between the three contestants, two balls on their front row and three balls on their back row. The same process is followed as for Round 1, with one more contestant being voted off.

Round 3 - Bin or Win

The ten balls from the two remaining contestants are mixed up with an additional killer ball. All eleven balls sit in front of them both, and they take it in turns to choose one ball to win (to be added to the jackpot), and one ball to bin. If a killer ball is chosen to 'win' then this knocks a zero off the cumulative value of the jackpot. This process is repeated five times. With the final ball being binned.

Final round - Split or Steal?

After the five balls have been chosen and the jackpot amount is set, each contestant has a choice between two remaining golden balls which say either 'Split' or 'Steal'.

- If both contestants choose a Split ball, the jackpot is split equally between them.
- If one contestant chooses a Split ball and the other chooses a Steal ball, the Stealer gets all the money and the Splitter gets nothing.
- If both contestants choose Steal balls, they both get nothing.

The players have a chance to speak with each other face to face before making their final choices. Ironically, Wikipedia describes this final predicament as being similar to a well known problem in game theory called Prisoner's Dilemma!

At 6pm I was taken to the studio to begin filming the show itself. My heart was pounding and I was really nervous as I walked onto the stage. I began talking to another woman at the side of me and one of the camera crew told us off like naughty school children talking in class (I didn't realise at the time that you weren't allowed to form alliances with the other contestants).

The game started, and I couldn't believe my luck. I had really high value balls, and I didn't have to be untruthful once. I worried that I wouldn't be believed, and was sure that I was going to be voted off, but I wasn't and so I ended up in the final with a woman called Gloria.

My intention all along had been to choose the Steal ball if I got this far, because I thought it was the only way you could guarantee you wouldn't be worse off than the other contestant. If I chose Steal and Gloria chose Spilt, I would win everything; if she chose Steal too, then we would both walk away with absolutely nothing. At the last minute, however, I changed my mind and chose the Split ball. I'd been influenced by a conversation at work a few days earlier. It had been no secret that I would be appearing on the show, and a senior officer and some of the prisoners had been talking about it. She'd asked what each of them would do if they were on the show and I had been surprised to hear that the majority would choose to Split; I had been one of the few who said they would opt for the Steal ball. I explained that it was the only way you could go on the show and guarantee that you wouldn't be the loser. One prisoner then shocked me by asking "But Miss, you lock thieves up every day for a living. How could you go on that show and choose the Steal ball and then walk back in here with any integrity?" How does someone answer that? I couldn't, and in those final seconds when I had to choose one ball, I chose to Spilt, deciding that my integrity was worth far more than the £17,650 jackpot, and that I wanted to set a good example to the people I worked with! Plus, if Gloria needed the money so badly that she would choose Steal, then she deserved to have it. To be honest, I guess there was also something about her that made me believe that what she was telling me was the truth. Gloria, I will always love you for our friendship and your kindness, and for choosing that Spilt ball. The Golden Girls rule!

The following day, I was still in shock as I started my planned travel adventure with Maggie, a girl from work I barely knew. We had trained in the gym together, but had never even had a coffee outside of work! During a spinning session we'd been talking and had discovered that we both wanted to go to New Zealand. I'd just blurted out that we should do it together, and Maggie had agreed! During this trip, I ticked off some things from my Bucket List that I had really thought were only a pipe dream.

I finally threw myself out of a plane at 12,000 feet, knowing that no matter how scared I was (and believe me I was scared stiff and on the verge of tears), this was something I had to do in order to become the person I was now on a mission to change into. Belief is a staggeringly powerful weapon, unless it's pondering the fear of being attached to an instructor by just a harness, and the worry of whether or not the 'chute would open, what would happen if the harness broke, and how much it would hurt if something did go wrong and I ended up hitting the floor and ultimately dying in agony.

I had chosen two songs that I had wanted to listen to for this parachute jump, the first being Madonna's *Are You Ready To Jump* as the plane was climbing higher and higher:

There's only so much you can learn in one place
The more that I wait, the more time that I waste
I haven't got much time to waste
It's time to make my way
I'm not afraid of what I'll face
But I'm afraid to stay
I'm going down my road and I can make it alone
I'll work and I'll fight till I find a place of my own

MYSELF, ME AND I

[Chorus]
Are you ready to jump
Get ready to jump
Don't ever look back oh baby
Yes, I'm ready to jump
Just take my hand
Get ready to jump

I was also planning to listen to Pink Floyd's *Learning to Fly* as I was free falling towards the earth below me:

Can't keep my eyes from the circling skies
Tongue-tied and twisted just an earth-bound misfit, I

Above the planet on a wing and a prayer,
My grubby halo, a vapour trail in the empty air,
Across the clouds I see my shadow fly
Out of the corner of my watering eye
A dream unthreatened by the morning light
Could blow this soul right through the roof of the night

There's no sensation to compare with this
Suspended animation, a state of bliss

Can't keep my mind from the circling skies
Tongue-tied and twisted just an earth-bound misfit, I

As I had shuffled to the edge of the doorway with my instructor, Gary told me to take out my earphones. I pressed pause, removed them and listened. Gary told me that we would rock backwards and forwards three times, and on the third time we would be flying.

With my heart pounding, I shuffled further forward, as instructed, put my earphones back in and switched my iPod back on, and now I was hanging out of the plane, with just the harness (that could snap at any minute!) to stop me falling. I felt Gary rock backwards once and then we were out of the plane. I'm afraid the words "Holy fucking shit, you bastard. You lied to me!" did leave my mouth at this point! But there was no going back. I was now plummeting towards the earth at 200 miles an hour! I took a deep breath and held it in, because otherwise the wind took your breath away, and I would be gasping for air. The free fall lasted only sixty seconds, but it seemed *much, much* longer. Once the 'chute opened up, I relaxed, and began to really enjoy the experience. This was the most amazing thing I had ever done! As we landed, and I was unhooked from Gary, I spun around and randomly hugged him. "That was the maddest thing I've ever done. Can we do it again?" And I would have if they hadn't been fully booked.

Over the next few weeks, as we travelled around Hong Kong, New Zealand and Australia, I continued to read the book that Stuart had given me.

The more I read, the more I began to understand myself truly for the very first time. This holiday was the perfect setting for my voyage of self-discovery. I'd made a huge step in the right direction by admitting my problems and deciding to finally take action to sort them out. However, I came to realise that Stuart, or anyone else for that matter, wouldn't be able to really help me until I began to help myself. The biggest thing I needed to do was to understand myself, to *really understand myself*, and to accept myself.

March, 2009

When I got home, my winnings cheque was waiting for me! I decided that I wanted to share my windfall with all the people in my life who had all been a support network for me, because money can't make you happy, but their support and love had been (was and is) priceless to me. I took all my close friends out for dinner and drinks and booked to take Mum on holiday to Spain, because she hadn't been able to afford to go abroad for many years. I bought my sister some lovely designer sunglasses (something she had always wanted), as well as a gold Oscar statue for being the World's Best Sister, for putting up with all the crap I'd given her over the years.

I had also wanted to get something for Ian, even if it was just a really nice bottle of wine, for his lifesaving hug, without which I may not have still been here, but I knew that would be weird. Because he had no idea at this stage just how monumental his act of kindness had been, or that it had probably saved my life. So instead of that, I gave a chunk of my windfall to a young boy who was the focus of a charity event we had at work. It was so rewarding to help someone who genuinely needed the money far more than I did, someone who had no choice about their circumstances and was so severely disabled. My money helped this child to get the stem cell treatment he desperately needed to change his life, making him more comfortable and prolonging his survival. He is also the one that made me realise that my own issues were insignificant. My problems had been created by me, myself. He had been born with terrible problems and yet he lived life to the full. Up until very recently, I hadn't been living, I had been merely existing!

April, 2009

During my next therapy session with Stuart, I started Cognitive Behavioural Therapy. At first, we worked on the importance of change and of letting go, and over the coming weeks Stuart set me tasks, such as completing a SWAT analysis (Strengths, Weaknesses, Opportunities and Threats), of my change process. He sent me home with worksheets to complete; I had to look at the different areas of my life, including Social, Work/Education, Financial, Emotional, Relationships etc and ask myself two questions:

1) Who do you want to be in this area?
2) What do you want to do in this area?

I answered these completely honestly and from the heart:

I don't want to be anyone else but me, I do want to be happy and I deserve to be happy, in all areas of my life. I am a good person and I push myself too hard to be perfect when it's not possible, because no one is perfect. I am currently a sad Jo Allott, and I really want to be a happy Jo Allott!

MYSELF, ME AND I

When I handed this to Stuart during our next session, he stood up from his desk and started dancing around the room! It was very random and funny, and I burst out laughing, before asking what on earth he was doing. "This called my Dance of Joy!" He chuckled, sitting back down.

Next, we moved on to behaviour experiments, and I nearly died when Stuart set the first one! He slid a pack of facial wet wipes across the table and told me to take my makeup off. I felt panic rising in my stomach. I never, ever left the house without having my full face on; surely he wasn't serious! "I can't Stuart; I need to go shopping when I leave here!" He simply repeated his instruction and told me that I had to go and do my shopping, as normal, but with no makeup on. I then needed to look at four things: "The result, the reflection, your revised belief and your final reflection."

I did as I was told, and it was very difficult, but when I'd completed this task, it felt amazing to realise that I had found the strength to do something which I would never have even contemplated doing a few months before.

Holy crap! Therapy is really awesome! Why people stigmatise it (as I had done myself in the past) I now had no idea! If you're ill you'll go to the doctors, won't you? If your car is broken you'll take it to the garage, won't you? Well therapy is doing just the same, but on a much bigger scale . . .

This was the first time that I could ever remember feeling truly good about myself. I liked it and really wanted it to continue. I saw Stuart later that week for my next session. We went through the results of the behaviour experiment together and I told him that I would like to read him the answers to his questions:

Result - *No one made a comment about me not wearing any make-up.*

Reflection - *I can do it, and need to start feeling better about myself.*

Revised belief - *It's not true that I have to look perfect all the time.*

Final reflection - *How I look makes no difference to the person I am.*

As I read my answers out to Stuart, he sat behind his desk with his hands clasped together and his chin resting upon them, wearing a huge smile on his face. "What are you smiling at?" He took his time to answer, looking at me carefully, but still smiling "You. I can't believe the difference in you, since you first walked through my door in January. It's everything about you. My goodness, I've never seen such a change in such a small amount of time. You're no longer the broken young woman you were. Even in the short time you have been visiting me, the difference is immense, right down to your aura." I told him that I was determined to do this, even though at first I hadn't been sure I could. Stuart told me I had a long way to go and that we were only at the beginning of a long road, but that he really thought we could do this together. I agreed and confirmed that I had never been so determined to do anything in my life. I was going get well again and I didn't care what I had to do or how long it was going to take. "I will do it, I know I will!" Stuart pointed out that he could see my determination in my face and my body language.

I didn't know it yet, but I would spend the next thirteen months working with Stuart, focusing mainly on Cognitive Behaviour Therapy techniques, but also completing thought diaries and other behavioural experiments that I never would have believed I could do.

JO ALLOTT

Daddy Dearest

August, 2009

I was visiting my mum and sister when I received a text from my dad, who had moved, with work, to live in Scotland about eighteen months earlier. The text said simply "Hi Jo, I'm really sorry to let you down, but the hotel I got you for next week has fallen through. Me and Jan have quit our jobs. We're leaving Scotland and moving back to England, due to an issue over Kerry's wedding. They messed up the leave and now say only one of us can get the time off to attend. Love Dad x."

I was no longer surprised by Dad letting me down or hurting my feelings. It was quite a bizarre moment and I think I surprised even myself because I had known that something would go wrong and now it had. I didn't even realise that I'd laughed out loud, until Kelli asked me what was so funny. "You know my birthday trip to Glasgow, to see U2 with my friend Andy? Well Dad has just told me that I can't have the hotel he arranged because they've both quit their jobs and are moving back to England because they can't get the time off work to attend Kerry's wedding!" Kelli asked me when I would learn, and reminded me that Dad had said that he wouldn't even come to my wedding with John, because he didn't want to spend time around my mum. And yet here they were, both quitting their jobs for Jan's granddaughter! I was *his daughter*! I didn't like hearing Kelli criticising Dad (as with most families, you can be critical of your relatives yourself, but feel defensive if someone else starts), but there really wasn't much I could say in his defence.

I stared blankly at the television screen, wondering what to do, and Kelli asked if I was OK. The problem was that of course I desperately wanted to go to see U2, my favourite band, but I knew that all the decent hotels would have been booked up months ago. Kelli moaned that she didn't know why I bothered with Dad "Anyone can be a father, but it takes a man to be a Dad. Why do you think I call him my Sperm Donor and her the Wicked Witch?" she laughed. But Kelli and I were totally different people. Kelli hadn't spoken to Dad since she had been about fourteen years old. She had been too young to even remember him being at home, so had never really developed the relationship with him that I had. But after thirty years of not questioning my father, this single text and what Kelli had just said to me, made me do just that. I stood up and told Mum and Kelli I was going for a walk. They were concerned about me, but I said I needed to think about things. As I walked around the village, it dawned on me that mine and my dad's entire relationship was and always had been one-sided; if I hadn't called him or visited him then I don't think we would have stayed in touch at all.

I had a million things whirling around my head, but I was processing them in a way that I never would have dreamed of. Previously, I would have been upset, hit the bottle, had a binge and questioned myself, asking what I had done to deserve this;

subconsciously blaming myself for my dad's behaviour. Now, I could be more detached. I wasn't happy, sure, but these things happened. It was out of my control and there wasn't anything I could do to change it. I got back to my mum's a short while later and smiled as I asked Kelli if I could borrow her laptop. I told her I was fine, but needed to sort out a hotel or we would be camping at a bus stop! She asked whether I was annoyed that he'd let me down again, and my reply surprised me as much as it did Kelli "What's the point of that, it won't change anything apart from making me feel bad." Kelli shook her head, as if to indicate that I was getting soft in my old age, but I was beyond caring. I wasn't going to get wound up about something that I couldn't control. Yes, Dad had let me down (again) on one of the few occasions I'd actually asked him to do anything for me, but this was only what I'd expected anyway. I scrolled through the internet, searching for some accommodation, but could only find something that was going to cost almost £500 for the two nights we would be in Glasgow! This would leave me £400 out of pocket because I couldn't ask Andy for a contribution. It wasn't his fault the accommodation had been changed, so I booked this up and just accepted the loss.

August 17th, 2009

The following week, Andy and I arrived in Scotland as planned. I was so excited that my favourite band was actually playing on my birthday and that we'd been lucky enough to get great tickets, right at the front of the stage. As we sat having dinner before the concert, my phone bleeped with a text from Dad.

I wondered if he'd actually remembered that it was my birthday for a change, but no such luck. As I sat shaking my head, Andy asked if I was OK. I said I guessed I was, but I just couldn't believe my dad sometimes. He asked what I meant and I read him Dad's message: "What is your mum doing discussing our business and that we let you down with the hotel?" That was all it said, and how the hell would I know what conversations my mum was having, I wasn't even there! He *had* let me down with the hotel and he hadn't even wished me a happy birthday! Andy tried to persuade me that I shouldn't let my dad spoil our evening, as we'd been looking forward to it for months, but I explained that it still hurt that he had been so quick to send such a negative and aggressive text. I wished I was more like Kelli, and really didn't care. "But that wouldn't be you Jo," Andy protested "You're not like that as a person. You make out you're this big rough and tough prison officer who doesn't care what people think of you, but it's as if when you take off your uniform you become a different person, the Jo that only those really close to you know. We know that the real you is a big softy who lets things get to her when she shouldn't and who over analyses and worries about things way too much." I knew Andy was right, and so switched my phone off without replying. Dad wasn't going to ruin this day for me.

The concert was amazing and we had a great time. I'd enjoyed it so much that at home a few days later I bought tickets to see U2 again in Cardiff the next weekend! Unfortunately, as I drove to the concert, I crashed my car. It was nothing serious, and I was fine, but as my car was taken away to be repaired I

220

made a decision to use that as an excuse not to attend Kerry's wedding the following weekend. Maybe it was wrong of me, but I decided I should look after myself and do what I wanted instead of doing something because I thought I should. I sent Dad a text and explained about the crash, and do you know what? He didn't even reply to ask if I was OK. He didn't know whether or not I'd been hurt, and he didn't bother to ask. It was only then that I realised just how little I must have actually meant to him. I also realised just how much I had grown as a person, and how much Stuart's therapy had changed me for the better. Because now, I was actually standing up to my father. He didn't know it yet, but I was no longer going to allow him to continue to hurt me. I saw that it didn't matter what I did, I could never change him or make him love me. I was finally recognising the truth – that all my years of anger, hurt, depression, self-loathing and self-abuse that had been caused by his comments to me as a child and by my unbridled desperation to please him and make him proud.

September 19th, 2009

I went back 'Up North' to visit my mum. It hadn't been long since my last visit, but it was her birthday on the Monday and I wanted to give her, her card and birthday gift. I explained to Mum and Kelli my decision about not attending the wedding but I don't think either of them believed me until I said I wasn't even going to visit Dad while I was home. He and Jan were now back in the house, not far from Mum's, that they'd kept on during their move to Scotland.

As I headed home, I felt really good about myself because I hadn't gone back on the decision I'd made. I know I should have just visited Dad and Jan, even for half an hour (just to keep the family peace), but I'd had enough of people treating me like crap and walking all over me. I wasn't going to let people do it to me anymore, and if that meant letting go of some of these negative influences in my life, then I would do just that. It was an uneasy and unfamiliar feeling, but also quite an empowering one. I lasted about four more days before I finally broke and rang Dad to see how he was. During our conversation, he told me how hurt he had been that I hadn't gone to see him. He knew I had been home because he'd seen my car. I couldn't believe what I was hearing. I listened politely, but was thinking to myself, *and just how often do you call me? How often do you visit me? NEVER, that's how often!* Did I say that? No, of course not. I was shocked enough to be thinking it, I couldn't have actually said it. Instead, I ended up apologising. Naughty Joanne, you let your Daddy down again, didn't you?!

October, 2009

Dad was soon to turn sixty, and during a call to him, Jan asked to speak to me and began to tell me of her plans for his special day. She was going to create an office for him in their smallest bedroom. I knew exactly where the conversation was going; she wanted me to put some cash towards the project. Otherwise, she would never have asked to speak to me in the first place. I jumped in before she could ask and said "What a good idea, I'll get him a printer." I'm sure that wasn't the answer she expected (more likely she was expecting me to go halves on everything), but a printer was what I offered. I found a really good printer/scanner/copier on eBay and arranged for it to be delivered direct to Dad's house because I would be working on his actual birthday. It all went horribly wrong! The printer turned up at my house two days before Dad's birthday, and I had no way of getting it up to him. I called and tried to explain this to Jan, but the conversation ended up completely out of control.

October 8th, 2009

I had had enough, and I finally lost my temper. I was done, but I was going to make sure I had my say at long last. I poured myself a large glass of red wine and wrote my dad a letter that I knew would end our relationship. I didn't care anymore. I wasn't the person I used to be and I didn't need to carry on taking rubbish from him or anyone else. I was a strong happy woman and I would be just fine without him.

Once I'd finished writing, I called Emma and asked her to come over after work to read the letter and give me her honest opinion.

Emma arrived shortly after 9pm and hugged me, saying "I'm really proud of you, because I know how hard this must have been for you to do." She then sat down with a glass of wine and the letter I had penned earlier that day. I didn't interrupt her, but watched her face with interest as she read, knowing there were things in there that she hadn't known about me. Finally, her response was "This is long overdue, but you still haven't been harsh enough. If you're going to do it, you may as well do it properly and get everything out!" I laughed and told her that this was enough to make sure I wouldn't hear from him again. (I knew my dad too well, besides there wasn't anything he could say about the letter, because every single word was the truth.) I asked Emma what she thought about me paying a courier to hand deliver it on his sixtieth birthday. Would that be too mean? I thought she was going to wet herself laughing, but she finally said "Jo, I love it! You've put up with twenty odd years of rubbish from that man, but do remind me never to cross you!" "I know! Happy Sixtieth Daddy Dearest!" We both laughed at this. The following day it cost me a silly amount of money to ensure my letter would be delivered in to Dad's hands, but it was worth every single penny. I had sent the letter with a birthday card which contained enough money to cover the cost of a printer.

Dad,

I am really sorry to be doing this and by mail on your birthday, but I am VERY upset, hurt and angry and need to say a few things that have been eating away at me for a long, long time.

Firstly, I am sorry about the printer which I got you for your birthday. I was unable to get it to you as it was delivered to my address and not to yours like I'd asked which was completely out of my control. So I went to the post office to try and get it posted to you (that's why I spoke to Jan on Thursday, so she knew what was going on and so I would not spoil your surprise), but because of the weight of the printer, it was going to cost over £20 to post it and would take anything between three and five days to deliver. I tried to explain this to Jan via text message and tell her that I would bring it up to you on my next day off and give it to you personally. The response I received was totally out of order, especially as I had tried my best to rectify the issue. I'm not sure if you know any of this, so I'll tell you exactly what happened.

As you know, I spoke to Jan. She then sent me a text telling me not to bother and that she would buy a printer, because you weren't going to be sixty next week and what a great birthday you were going to have! She told me to put the printer back on eBay (which I was very hurt by). I sent a text back saying it would be silly to buy another printer, and asking her whether she thought I'd planned this and what did she want me to do, as I was working all weekend! All I got in response to this was "Done, sorted." I certainly didn't want an argument with anyone, but at this point I was very angry and did say things which when I read them back may have come across as what I intended at all. My response was "Whatever, I'm not going to argue over something so silly, and I will put a cheque in his birthday card to cover the cost of the printer." The response I got to this was from you??? And said "Silly Sixtieth. Don't bother to send it, it will be sent back, Dad!" I find it hard to believe that this was you, because this would have spoilt your surprise, but if it was, then I'm sorry you feel that way as I would never have done this intentionally. I decided after this that I wasn't going to respond again, as I didn't want to bounce texts back and forth about something that I had no control over. Then a while later I received another text which simply said "No answer???" Again I didn't answer.

I am sorry but I do not deserve to be treated this way, there have been many things over the years that have been said and done which have really upset me! I have never spoken to you about these because you are my dad; and I have wanted to keep the peace. But, I can't go on like this and keep quiet any longer, if this means that you then refuse to speak to me, then that is something I will have to live with, but I have to get them off my chest now.

Do you realise that the only time we ever speak or see each other is when I call or visit you? I have lived in Milton Keynes for over eight years and you have never been to see me? (Well, apart from my Passing-Out Parade and then you rushed straight off home, not even coming to my house for a cup of coffee.) Even when I was very ill in hospital for two weeks having my appendix removed, it was me that called you. When you were in hospital yourself, I was the last person to find out about it! I am your daughter, I should have been told right away, not by phone after midnight as some afterthought.

Jan has really upset me with this issue of your birthday. Do you know, I can't remember the last time I received a birthday card on time from you, but I have never said anything, no matter how upset I've been over this because it is you and I have just accepted it. This year I received a text message from you on my thirty first birthday, asking me why my mum was discussing you and your business, and the fact that you had let me down with the hotel. You did let me down with the hotel and I was over £400 out of pocket after I booked another one, but did I once complain or even say anything to you about that? No I didn't, because I wanted to keep the peace. Do you know you never even wished me happy birthday when you were texting me? All you cared about was you.

There's something else I feel you should know. For over eighteen years I have been ill, are you aware of that??? I am just curious about how well you actually know your own flesh and blood. For over eighteen years I have suffered with bulimia and do you know what started that? I was twelve years old and I remember my dad saying to me that I was getting fat. He made me get on to the scales and said he would give me £1 for every pound in weight I lost . . . do you remember that? Because I do. When Mum discovered I was ill, and found out what had caused this, I thought she would kill you. But I made her promise never to say a word to you and to help me get well again. That illness has probably taken away the chance of me ever having my own children, and all because I wanted to be thin, beautiful and loved by my dad.

But the biggest thing that sticks in my mind is when I was going to get married. You and Jan sat me down and you said to me that you wouldn't be able to go to my wedding as you couldn't spend a week at the same place as my mum and sister; you could have chosen another hotel and just been there for

227

my wedding. Again, I never said a word about this. Mum and Kelli were in the same situation and they were willing to do it for me, without so much as a hesitation or thought that you and Jan would be there. Yet this year, when your wife's granddaughter was getting married and you couldn't both get time off work to attend, what happened? Yes, that's right; you both quit your jobs and moved back from Scotland so you could be there. Can you imagine how hurt I am that you would do something like that for her, yet you would not have even have been at my wedding? That is the real reason I didn't come to Kerry's wedding, because it made me realise once and for all how much more you think of Jan's side of the family. I am just the remaining jigsaw piece from what was your past life, aren't I?

There is so much more I could say, but there is no point going on and on. I know the above has done enough and that I will probably never hear from you again. So all I can say now is, no matter what, you will always be my dad and I will always love you, but I need to think of me first now. I will leave it with you, should you wish to contact me and if not, then be happy and have a nice life.

Jo x

I didn't hear from my dad until the following Thursday. As I opened my mail box, I was greeted by a white envelope with his hand writing on it. I wasn't sure what to expect, but it certainly wasn't what I received! I put the envelope on my coffee table while I plucked up the courage to open it. The adrenaline was pumping around my body and I was nervous and sweating in anticipation. Finally, I picked it up and tore it open. Inside the envelope was the letter that I had sent him and his unopened birthday card. That was it. Again I wasn't even worth so much as a response. That told me everything that I needed to know, and finally allowed me to let Dad go and to move on once and for all. I still have the letter and the unopened birthday card, which has the printer cash inside it, but this will never be opened. Even if I become desperate for money at some point in my life, I will never, ever touch this.

It has now been almost four years since I last spoke to or saw anything of my dad and of course that it still deeply upsetting to me. I do wonder if he ever thinks of me, or has any regrets in his life, because none of his family speaks to him, which I think is really sad. But I also meant what I said in my letter, that I will always love him because I am his daughter, no matter what, and without him I wouldn't be alive. I know you might think I'm mad, but if he ever needed me, even if it was to give him one of my kidneys, I would be there for him! Because believe it or not, his daughter is really a nice person, who he should (could) be so proud of....

I would however like to extend on my letter to him, but not in a negative way, because I wish him no harm or malice. *Dad, if you ever read this book, I have some advice for you in your next life.*

How to really love a child: *Firstly be there for them, let them bang on pots and pans, say yes to them as often as you can, encourage them to be* *silly, and giggle with them a lot! Remember how small they really are and search out the positives in them, while keeping the gleam alive in their eyes. Dance in the rain together in your pyjamas, teach them about feelings, realise how important it is to be a Dad to your child. Plan to build a tree house together. ALWAYS remember that what you say to your child really does make a lasting impression! Most importantly, express your love A LOT, because children really are miraculous gifts that you are privileged to receive.*

Time to say Goodbye

Where this new found inner strength had come from, I had absolutely no idea; I had now been in therapy for approximately ten months, and the transformation that I had gone through in this time was incredible. It felt as if when I had first started my journey I had been a caterpillar who had then gone into a cocoon and was now emerging the other side as a beautiful butterfly, spreading her wings out wide for the very first time and learning to fly. Now, at last, when I looked in the mirror I liked the reflection I could see staring back at me. I was finally the beautiful, happy, healthy, young woman that I had wanted to be for so very, very long. I had done it; I had achieved what I wanted to and kept the promise I'd made to myself.

The thing that concerned me was going it alone, because that was my next big challenge! I knew I should end my therapy sessions with Stuart, because I realised that I no longer needed them, but I didn't really want to end them, just in case I couldn't cope alone and was destined to return to the person that I had once been. Stuart had become my 'Stewie-bear'; he was like the teddy bear that you have as a child to which you tell your deepest darkest secrets, because they'll listen and never say a word to judge you. So I was now in a quandary about what I was going to do, because the last thing in the world that I would ever want was Myself or Me coming back out to play. I attended my next session a few days later and I was totally honest with Stuart, explaining my concerns about the risk of going backwards and how much that petrified me. Stuart agreed that I was strong enough to start moving away from our sessions, so we decided that the best course of action was to reduce them from weekly to every other week, with regular assessments and feedback on how this was working out for me. We would then reduce to monthly sessions and then finally I would be done. I was to be weaned away slowly from what had become my safety blanket. This approach worked very well for me. I saw Stuart gradually less and less, and when anything stressful happened over those next few months, I was able to face it and deal with it like the normal functioning person I now was! It felt truly amazing! At the beginning, I knew had my next therapy session lined up to support me, even if it was still a couple of weeks away, and I knew that I would be able to talk about whatever the issue had been and then it let it go, because it was gone, it was done and had been dealt with rationally. My final session with Stuart was due to be in March, 2010.

February 11th, 2010

I was at the hairdressers, having my hair done because I was due to fly out to Hungary the following day with my friend Sylvie, who was Hungarian herself. A few years earlier, Sylvie had been my lodger for a while, and we'd been great friends ever since. She'd been inviting me to go out to Hungary for years, but our schedules always seemed to clash. I was really looking forward to what I was sure would be a great trip because I would be seeing the real Hungary, not the tourist Hungary, which was an opportunity that always appealed to me when I visited somewhere new. My mobile began to ring, and normally I would have let it go to voicemail because I was busy, but some instinct told me I should answer Kelli's call. "Jo, please don't panic, but Mum's been taken into hospital." I must have sounded quite alarmed as I asked Kelli what she meant, why I shouldn't panic and what on earth was going on, because the hairdresser stopped cutting my hair, tapped me on the shoulder and ushered me into the back of the shop so I could have some privacy.

I could hear Kelli crying down the phone, but she wouldn't answer me! In sheer frustration, I shouted down the phone "Kelli, just tell me what is going on!" I knew that my mum hadn't been very well for a few weeks, with repeated chest infections, but that was no surprise because she'd been working in a butcher's shop which kept both the front and back doors open all year around, even in the winter. I had told her a few weeks before not to go back into work until she was well again, but she wouldn't listen to me. She got very little sick pay, because she only worked part time hours, so she told me she couldn't afford to be absent. I had even at one point offered to pay her wages so that she would take the time off and get herself well again, but my mother is a stubborn, proud mare and would not even contemplate this as an option. *I wonder which daughter takes after her on this one (Oooooh, I know, pick me, pick me!)* Kelli finally spoke "Mum went to the doctors a couple of hours ago and the receptionist called the doctor though into the waiting room soon as she arrived. He took one look at Mum and called an ambulance right there and then!" OK .

. . so now I knew this was more serious than I had originally thought, and Kelli had been telling me not to worry! Kelli said she wasn't sure what they thought it was, but it could be her heart because they'd rushed her away in the ambulance with the lights flashing and the siren blaring. Mum had contacted her sister because she lived closest to the hospital and she knew Kelli was at work, and Aunty Sharon had just called Kelli. "Right," I snapped, "I'm on my way up. I'll be there as quickly as I can!" I hung up and quickly explained to my hairdresser what had happened. Then I ran out of the salon with half a hair cut that I didn't even stop to pay for.

As I ran to my car, I sent Emma a text asking her to sort out things at work for me and telling her that I'd be in touch again as soon as I had an update. I gave Sylvie a quick call to let her know that I wouldn't be able to fly out with her the following day. Right now, though, none of that mattered, all that mattered was my mum. When I got home, I wasted time flapping around in sheer terror, because I wasn't thinking straight. Suddenly, I heard my front door open, which alarmed me as I didn't have a lodger at that time. I stuck my head around the corner as the door swung open, to see that it was Emma, who had been in the area and had my spare house keys on her. She walked straight up to me and gave me a hug before frog marching me into lounge. "Jo, sit bloody down! You are going nowhere in that state, because you're not safe to drive! If I have to drive you up to Mansfield myself then that's what we will do, but you're certainly not driving until you've chilled out a little!" Typical Emma, she had always been one to depend on in a situation like this. She then stomped off into the kitchen and came back with a cup of tea for each of us. I did as I was told, and calmed myself down enough so I could make the journey home by myself. Emma told me not worry about work and that she would sort that out for me, she just wanted me to promise to drive safely and carefully. I did, until I got on the M1; then my foot really hit the floor. The journey usually took me about an hour and forty five minutes, but on this occasion I knocked half an hour off that time. I just needed to get home to my mum as quickly as I could.

I drove straight to the hospital, not knowing where Mum actually was until I'd called Kelli. As I walked into the ward and saw her for the first time, I was shocked by Mum's appearance. She looked so pale and ill, and although she was only fifty seven, she looked at least ten years older. It turned out she'd developed pneumonia, which was further complicated by the fact that she only had one fully functioning lung. As the days passed, Mum deteriorated and her kidneys began to fail, so she was taken into critical care. I really thought we were going to lose her.

We spent as much time as we could with Mum, but we couldn't be at the hospital all the time. I'd been to the gym for a workout when on my return I was told by the nurses that Mum was having difficulties. I hurried down the corridors to the intensive care department to see Kelli running towards me, crying. I now feared the worst but I couldn't get any sense out of my sister! I went to the nurse's station and asked what was going on and where Mum was. Suddenly, I was aware that I could hear my mum crying, just like I had when I'd been a little girl in my hospital bed. I spun round on my heels to see that the bed behind me had the curtains drawn around it. I headed straight over, not knowing what would be waiting for me behind those green curtains. The nurse behind me was telling me that I couldn't go in, but I protested "That's my mum! Just you try and stop me!" As I opened the curtains, I saw that the bed was surrounded by doctors and nurses in green scrubs and masks. I had never seen so many people tending to one person. A doctor looked up at me and said, "Miss, you really can't be in here!" but mum had seen me enter and was begging me not to leave her alone. I had never seen Mum like this, and it was both heartbreaking and terrifying. I glared at the doctor and stated firmly "If you think I am leaving my mum when she's like this, you have another thing coming. Just get on with what you're doing, and I'll keep out of your way!" With that, I grabbed Mum's hand and told her to focus on me and not on what the doctor was doing.

Mums vital statistics were off the chart at this point and all the machines were bleeping loudly with their alarms ringing. Mum ended up having a right heart catheterization with no pain relief while wide awake! I was holding her hand and trying to distract her, but it was difficult to distract myself from what was happening; I never want to witness anything like that ever again. Ever the analytic, as I sat and held Mum's hand, I realised that I was now an even stronger woman than I'd thought I was. Kelli and I are two very different daughters. Kelli is the type of daughter who would call or text mum daily, even if she had nothing to say, just to confirm that she loved her, in case that was her last opportunity to say it. I'm not like that. Mum knows I love her, but I don't need to tell her every day. I'm the one who would deal with things head on, and after this experience, I thought I wouldn't be fazed by anything else that life chose to throw in my direction.

Throughout Mum's illness, Emma was an absolute rock of support, calling me every day to see how I was and if I needed anything. I had left Milton Keynes with almost nothing but the shirt on my back, and she'd even offered to go and get me some clothes from home and drive them up the motorway for me. I couldn't have wished for a better friend and thanked my lucky stars that I had her in my life. Mum remained in critical care for another week before her health started to improve. This time was incredibly stressful for me, naturally, and I did feel like binging at times, of course I did. Binging was what I had always done to cope with my life. But now I was strong enough to fight it, and I was so proud of myself that I never broke and gave in to the temptation.

While I was staying at Mum's, I had to deal with her day to day affairs, like paying her bills. Someone had to, and as I was the eldest, and the more sensible one with money, it fell to me. One morning, I opened one of Mum's letters to find a credit card statement. I couldn't believe my eyes when I saw the balance, particularly as Mum had always been the type of woman to say, as we were growing up, "If you can't afford it you don't have it and if you want it that badly you save for it!" She hadn't believed in credit cards. I had no choice but to confront Mum and ask her how on earth she'd built up a debt of £2,500. I was devastated to find out that most of the money had been spent on food, medication and general living expenses, because Mum's wages were so meagre and she was struggling to survive. It really made me put my own life in perspective. I would think nothing of spending £500 on the latest pair of Gucci shoes simply because I could, and yet my mum was struggling to be able to afford to eat and I didn't even know. I told her not to worry, that I would take care of it, but I also made her promise me that she would ask for my help if this kind of thing ever happened again.

Once mum was well enough, I went back home to Milton Keynes, back to work and to my life in general. My next visit to see Stuart was on March the eleventh, and this was to be my last. I knew if I could cope with everything I'd just been through, then I was ready for this clean break. Finally, I was ready to go it alone.

I'd been back at work for a few weeks when a colleague of mine asked me if Emma and I had fallen out. I was really puzzled and asked him what on earth he was talking about. Of course we hadn't, why would he even ask? He apologised, but I wasn't satisfied with his answer, and asked him what he'd heard. Apparently, he had heard Emma telling someone else that if she had passed her JSAC, then she would have got the promotion that I had been given, because she was better at the job than I was. (JSAC is a job simulation that prison staff complete in order to prove that they're competent to carry out certain roles, before they are eligible for promotion.) I couldn't believe what I was hearing and I didn't want believe it, not Emma, surely not. But then I thought back to when Emma had been given a temporary promotion a few years before. The first thing I had done was take her out to dinner to celebrate. When my promotion had come through more recently, I'd suggested that we go out, but she'd told me she wasn't in the right frame of mind. I had assumed she was disappointed not to have been promoted herself, but hadn't thought any more about it. I put what I had heard out of my mind, because Emma was my friend, she was like the big sister I'd never had. I was sure she wouldn't talk so negatively about me.

Emma's JSAC score had been so close to a pass that she decided to appeal and was successful. I was really happy for her. She was then promoted too, and we were going to be working alongside each other. I predominately worked on the First Night Centre, and Emma worked mainly on the Induction Wing. Although we had got along so well for so many years as colleagues and the closest of friends, as our paths crossed in these new roles it became clear that we each had very different management styles, but I didn't say anything to Emma.

May, 2010

On my first day back after my main leave break, my manager had a real go at me in the staff briefing because we hadn't met the Wing Cell Searching Target for that month. After the meeting, I asked if I could speak to him privately in his office and told him that it had been inappropriate for him to shout at me in front of all the staff. I reminded him that this was my first day back after three weeks of leave, and that he should have spoken to the manager who had actually failed to achieve this target, rather than to me. I had no idea that this was Emma, until she burst into my office later that day, ranting and raving that I'd dropped her in the shit! I explained that I'd taken a bollocking in the lunchtime briefing in front of all the wing staff for something that had had nothing to do with me because I'd been away. I hadn't known it was her, but I wasn't going to take the blame for something that wasn't my fault. "You could have told me what to do," Emma argued, "You're supposed to be my friend but you've never helped me since I've been on here. You were promoted thirteen months before me and you should have told me what I needed to do!" I couldn't believe she was blaming me for this. I told her she wasn't the type of person to take instructions from me anyway, and because she had previously been promoted on a temporary basis I'd assumed that she had known what to do, or that she would have asked for my help if she hadn't. Not too long ago, I would have apologised and agreed that it was my fault, but the new Jo was standing up for herself, though at a cost. Not long after this confrontation, Emma began to distance herself from me and our friendship.

I'm not sure I noticed at first, because I was so busy. I felt I'd become stale at Ribbleton, and so was looking at other prisons to secure a permanent Senior Officer post. Initially, I applied for five posts all over the country. My first choice was HMP Forby because this would get me closer to Mum so that I could help to look after her more easily, and I would have looked for somewhere to live in the Derbyshire Dales, which would have suited my love of the outdoors. Next came HMP Mandiville, Loyesford and Graterford, which were all around Buckinghamshire. I was already established in the area and wouldn't have to move house. Mandiville would have suited my love of working with young offenders, Loyesford was similar to what I was currently doing but would offer more responsibility, and Graterford was a therapeutic jail which offered something completely new and would present interesting challenges (although I decided it wasn't for me once I'd visited). Lastly, there was Thorpearch in the beautiful South West. I loved the location, and would have been very happy to move there, until I realised the property costs and that there would be no financial support to help me relocate.

So, having visited all five establishments, I continued with my applications for Forby, Mandiville and Loyesford. The post in Mandiville was subsequently pulled, leaving me with two interviews. I was successful at both boards but then the Juvenile Unit was to be closed down at Forby, so I was left with Loyesford in the end.

The last eight weeks at Ribbleton were so depressing for me. It was as if a huge grey cloud hung over the gate as I walked through it, sapping the life out of me. Staff morale in the jail was at rock bottom, and I couldn't wait to leave and accept a fresh challenge. I had also begun to notice that Emma was becoming very distant. She very rarely answered or returned my calls and texts, and barely spoke to me at work.

I had no idea why, but her attitude towards me seemed to have completely changed, or maybe I was just being paranoid. I spoke with Becky at length about the situation, because it really upset me. Emma and I had been so close, and she had been such a great friend when mum had been ill. Becky told me that Emma had changed towards her too, a few years earlier, and she hadn't any idea why either. But Emma was supposed to be my closest friend. I had done nothing to upset her that I could think of. I'd asked her if she was OK, but she had avoided giving me an answer. I didn't know what else to do.

It was only when she didn't send me a birthday card or even wish me happy birthday that year, I realised that I wasn't being paranoid at all; something was wrong, and the dynamics of our friendship had been drastically changed.

I had sent an email around the jail saying I would be having a leaving drink on 4th September. Of course I still invited Emma, but I didn't get a reply. Early on the evening of the planned get together, a text came through from Emma, "Hi Jo, I won't be coming to your leaving drink. I feel our friendship has distanced since you lied to me two years ago." I couldn't believe what I was reading!

Two years previously, I had started dating someone at work. Although I'd said this was something I would never do, we had both gone through a similar breakup at the time and it sort of just happened. We decided to keep the relationship quiet because I guess we both knew we were on the rebound, and we worked together, so we thought we'd see if anything came of it first before we told anyone else. Emma had asked me directly if I was seeing him, and I had told her I wasn't. The day after, however, I was feeling so awful about not having been honest with Emma that I'd apologised and told her the truth. Emma had slapped me around the head and told me never to lie to her again, and then told me that she hoped it worked out with him because he was a nice guy and I deserved someone nice! There had been no apparent change in the relationship between Emma and me over the next eighteen months or so, so I knew this excuse was bullshit, and I told her so. I believed our relationship had begun to change from the moment I had stood up to her during the confrontation in my office, but I'll never know the true reasons (though I do have my suspicions and theories). Emma decided to end our friendship, but she really hurt me by doing so.

The thought of this lost relationship hurt me very, very much, and I binged (before my leaving do) for the first time for many, many months. After the purge, I felt the guilt that I always did, but this time it was magnified ten-fold, because I had worked so very hard to get where I was and I was so disappointed in myself for having allowed Emma's text affect me that much. I was even more disappointed in myself because I hadn't broken and given in over losing my relationship with my dad, or even when my mum had been critically ill. But I suppose I had at least understood the reasons for those traumas, whereas here I didn't understand at all. It felt crap to have been abandoned by someone who was supposed to have been my closest friend for over six years.

She'd used a rubbish excuse; we'd been through so much worse together over the years, and she had never walked away from me, even in my darkest of days. To do so like this, now, well I just couldn't understand it.

I struggled to be me my usual bubbly self at my leaving party and Becky asked what was wrong. I showed her Emma's text. "Jo, that's total rubbish, and you know it! You said exactly the same to me too, because I was there when she asked you. Have I walked away? No, because you're right, your business is your business and you'll tell people when you're ready to. If she's used that has an excuse after six and a half years of friendship, all I can say is that she was never a genuine friend in the first place." Becky always had a great way of knowing how to cheer me up, and at least I had her. Her friendship really was unconditional, full of love and support for me.

I ended up ditching my own leaving party early because just the week before I had managed to arrange a great last-minute holiday. As I sat on the plane at Luton, I decided to give Emma what she wanted. I wasn't going to let her undo all the hard work that I had done to get to where I was now. This evening had been a blip, but I would start all over again tomorrow. As I went to turn my phone off before departure, I pulled up her contact details and deleted her numbers and her email address. I haven't spoken to her since, other than to politely request via work email that she return my spare house keys, and to cordially say hello when I've bumped into her at the odd social function. I just let her go, because there wasn't anything I could do about it; I let Emma go, along with my dad, along with John, Paul and George, along with my anger about Jennie's suicide, but most importantly, I let her go along with Myself and Me, because all that mattered now was the people that really wanted to be in my life and would support me in staying happy and healthy.

I spent the next week in Corfu, relaxing and taking in the sun with my friend Josie, having some much needed girlie fun before returning home to start my new job at Loyesford Prison. I had made a conscious decision that this move was also going to be a fresh chapter and a new start in my life. Throughout my time at Ribbleton, I had always worried about what people thought of me, whether I had upset them, and how much they liked me. I no longer cared about any of this inconsequential, shallow, superficial nonsense. Maybe because I was finally happy within myself, my attitude now was that if people liked me and wanted to be a part of my life then that was great, but if they didn't, then I would happily wave them goodbye and wish them well, just like Emma. I was also determined I was going to start Loyesford with the focus on work. I didn't need to be the social butterfly that I had always been, attending every leaving drink or night out, nor did I need masses of friendships at work, because these were not genuine life-long friendships. Most of the time, people would be nice to your face and then would be gossiping behind your back, in the next breath - so thanks but no thanks, Loyesford was going to be my place of work only, because I had all the true friendships in my life that I needed.

JO ALLOTT

Learning to Fly

September 20th, 2010

When my alarm woke me at 5.30am, it dawned on me that I was no longer a Prison Officer working at Ribbleton; I was now a Senior Officer at Loyesford. I knew just a couple of people who would also be working there. There was another Senior Officer and her husband who I'd worked with many years ago, when I'd first joined the prison service. She had been interviewed on the same day as me and we'd bumped into each other at the gate. We'd both been successful. And there was Trevor, who I had met at my Group Four interview in 2002. I'd remained friends with him and his lovely wife Gill ever since. As I walked through the gate for the first time, I felt quite nervous, but I needn't have worried. I was met by the Training Manager, who welcomed me to the team at Loyesford with one of the hugest smiles I've ever seen. Within seconds of being through the gate, I could sense how much more relaxed the place was, the staff genuinely seemed happy and smiling, which is something I hadn't seen for a while. I'd become so unhappy at Ribbleton towards the end, that I'd contemplated leaving the prison service altogether, so it was very refreshing to experience a different atmosphere, and it instantly put me at ease.

The day started off with all the necessary paperwork, followed by a quick tour of the prison, before I attended the Governor's morning meeting, which was something I had never attended before. I sat at the end of the table as the room slowly filled up with all the senior managers. Then a middle aged gentleman stood up, and walked around the table towards me. He extended his hand, and introduced himself as Pete. This completely freaked me out - the Number One Governor walking over to me, personally introducing himself and welcoming me to his management team! I couldn't quite believe it. At Ribbleton, my last Number One was addressed as Governor or Sir, so I couldn't quite take on board this informal approach, but I knew I'd made the right decision in taking this job.

I was given an induction programme to follow for the next two weeks, to ensure I was competent in the roles that I had not yet performed. I had been told that I would be managing numerous areas of the jail, the First Night Centre and Induction, which I was already familiar with, as well as Resettlement, C wing (normal population), and F wing (vulnerable prisoners). Along with these specific areas of responsibility, I would also be required to cover areas such as Reception and the Orderly Officer role, managing the day to day logistics of the prison and taking control of any incidents that happen; ensuring, for example, that the jail is staffed appropriately. I was nervous about all the extra responsibilities, and soon realised that I had been micro managed at Ribbleton. Now, I would have to make decisions for myself. The first Friday, on my first day in the Orderly Officer role, I was to shadow another Senior Officer (SO) called Simon. I met him for the first time that morning, and he scared the hell out of me. He was a huge, strapping man, well over six feet tall. Built like a rugby player, with a deep booming voice, he made me feel so tiny by his side that I wondered if I could really take on this responsibly, when I felt so out of my depth.

For the entire morning, I watched Simon like a hawk and tried to absorb everything he did, because he had told me that he would be handing me the reins that afternoon for the whole weekend, GULP! The morning was very quiet though, so I wasn't able to learn very much at all. Simon laughed and handed me the keys and handcuffs straight after lunch, poking me in the ribs and saying "You're it!" In truth, I was shitting myself. What if I screwed up? What if I made the wrong decision? What if someone got hurt because of something I did or said? Not *much* pressure then Jo, I was thinking, but I didn't voice my concerns. "So what's the regime on a Friday afternoon then?" I asked. "Don't worry," Simon said, "I'm breaking you in gently, there's just canteen and Muslim service." Phew, I was thinking, that didn't sound too bad. I asked him what we needed to do first. "What's the one thing that you haven't yet done today?" Simon laughed, going on to explain to my puzzled expression "I'll give you a clue; I've done it twice this morning." Aah, so that was it. He was keeping score was he? I grabbed the kettle and two mugs, just as the PE SO bounced into the office "That was good timing! Mine's white with no sugar Red," he interjected. I knew he was referring to my bright red hair, but told him he was a cheeky sod and that my name was Jo. I was quickly beginning to realise that Loyesford was full of banter between the staff and I would have to stand my ground!

I made the drinks and realised that Mark, the PE SO, had disappeared. Asking Simon where he had gone, I was put out to be told he'd probably gone back up to the gym. I tutted loudly, "Seriously? Cheeky bugger asks me to make him a drink and then walks off, how rude! I'm tempted to ring him and give him what for!" Simon burst out laughing "You daren't!" he challenged. You just watch me, I thought. I grabbed the coffee and stomped up to the gym, deciding that rather than phoning, I should make Mark drink his coffee, even if it was getting cold. I bowled through the door and slammed the drink down on his desk. "If you ask me to make you a drink, then you should be polite and drink it. OK?" I stated. Without giving him the chance to speak, I headed back over to the main wings, giggling to myself. As I walked back in, Simon was on the phone laughing. As he put it down, he gave me a Hi-Five! "Well done girl, you'll fit in here perfectly! That was Mark on the phone; you scare the hell out of him. I love it, you're like a female version of me, boy, are you and me going to have some fun!" I came to realise later that despite his intimidating presence, Simon was really a giant teddy bear, so maybe we *were* quite similar! At the time, I just laughed, knowing that a few years ago, I would never have had the confidence to behave like that without a stiff drink or two inside me, especially with someone that I didn't know. But I wanted to set my precedent right from the off - I wasn't going to be a pushover.

My first weekend as Oscar One (Duty Manager) was totally manic. I arrived at work on the Saturday morning to be faced with my first ever death in custody, which threw me straight in at the deep end and earned me the nickname The Angel of Death. These trying challenges I was faced with early on really developed my management skills to the max. Outside of work, my love of cooking was at its peak. Miraculously, I had managed to turn my past food demons in to my new passion; it was the one good thing to come out of my eating disorder. A group of my girlfriends and I hosted our own Come Dine With Me Evenings, and after I won the fun competition for the third time, one of them said I should apply for MasterChef because my food was "That good!" . . . so I did. A few weeks later, I received a call from the BBC and had to do a phone audition. I worried that I'd been rather arrogant at that stage, though, with some of the answers I'd given. For example, when asked "Do you think you can win the competition?" my response was, "There would be no point in me applying if I didn't think that." I was sure I wouldn't hear anything from them after this.

February, 2011

Over the last few months, I had settled well in to my new role and had enjoyed being at work. I had become very close to Simon, particularly after one weekend when I was again working as Oscar One and a huge snow storm started. I had known that I would never get home through the winding lanes in my little car, and so had been looking for a local hotel when Simon told me I was daft and that I could use his spare room. Moments later, the Duty Governor put a call out for me attend his office with the staff detail. It was decided to put the jail into Patrol State and send home the staff that lived some distance away, because of the inclement weather. As we were working through the detail of the staff on duty, the Number One Governor, Pete, phoned and said that he could be in the jail with fifteen minutes if needed, and even on the wings unlocking cell doors if necessary. He also informed us that he had five spare beds if any of the staff were stuck. This was the team ethos throughout Loyesford Prison as a whole, right the way from the Number One Governor down to the admin staff. I had very rarely even seen any Suits at Ribbleton, but every day, Pete personally went to each area of the jail and spoke to his staff; this hands-on management style really made Loyesford a great place to work.

June, 2011

It was 7am, and I had nearly finished the first night-shift of my third set of nights (7 on, 7 off). I was waiting at the gate for the day staff to arrive when a call came across the radio asking for urgent medical assistance in C2-04. I knew the guy in that cell was on suicide watch, and ran across the prison campus as quickly as I could, not knowing what I would find. I entered the cell to see more blood than I had ever seen in my life; you couldn't see the cell floor for all the blood. I was convinced that this would be my second death in custody, and even the paramedics had a 'no chance here' expression on their faces when they arrived a few minutes later. Miraculously, thanks to the quick actions of the night staff, the prisoner actually survived.

Later that day, back on night-shift, a prisoner was sent out to hospital with severe alcohol withdrawal.

Unfortunately, the hospital weren't able to treat him because of his refractory behaviour. When he returned to the prison, there was a half-tied bandage around his head and blood was running down his face. I made a decision to keep on one of the escorting staff, rather than release them from duty, as I knew he would need to go back to the hospital at some point in the night. By 5am, I had the paramedics back in the jail. As I was helping the prisoner into the back of the ambulance, he fell and landed on my right hand, which connected with the corner of the steps. I'd fractured a bone in my hand, but didn't realise for over a week, just thinking that it was badly bruised.

By Wednesday, after such a difficult start to the week, I was dreading what would be thrown at me as I walked through the gate, but it was to be what I would describe as a quiet night, until . . . when I returned from doing my 5.15am rounds, I was met by Ali, one of the night staff. "Here, Trappy (her pet name for me!), I can't get a response from a guy on A4 landing and he's lying funny." I asked her what she meant, and to show me. I followed her up the stairs, and as I opened the observation panel, I knew he was dead. I could see the blood pooled in his legs, but from where I was standing, and the position he was in, I thought it had been a natural death, with him falling over after a heart attack or something.

By this time one of the other night officers, Carole, had arrived, and I entered the cell. As I approached the man, I could see a ligature around his neck, but it was unlike anything I'd seen before. He had made a tourniquet (which he had put in his mouth) and twisted it tightly and until he'd successfully strangled himself. While we had only been sitting yards away. I dealt with the situation as I needed to, but this really was turning into the week from hell. I had to drag myself back into work on the Thursday evening and was praying that the rest of the week would be more stable. No such luck! I couldn't believe what I was faced with, and that I actually coped with everything that was put in my path. Eighteen months earlier, I would probably have had a nervous breakdown if I'd had to deal with only half of this week's incidents. Boy was I ready for my trip to America the following week! The only good thing about this week was that I received a call from MasterChef, inviting me for an audition in September.

July, 2011

In 2006, when I'd been in Jamaica with John, were we'd met some 'loud Americans' who were on their honeymoon. Initially I wasn't sure what to make of them, but we soon became good friends after I really got to know them, and I loved to visit them. Sarah and Ant have the most amazing log cabin home hidden away in six acres of wood in Birdsboro, Pennsylvania. It is my secret piece of heaven, so unspoilt that you could sit out on the porch and watch the fireflies dancing in the woods at night. I'd already visited them three times in the past year, when a planned trip to see U2 in Philadelphia fell through but I decided I'd use it as an excuse to visit them again anyway. I had enjoyed three wonderful weeks with them, and was incredibly relaxed, even if a little jet lagged on my first day back at work.

I was doing my rounds, and had just entered F Wing to do my management checks when I was met by Lee, the Residential Governor. Lee was one of the most sarcastic men I've ever met, though I gave as good as I got. He wasn't your typical Governor, as he was a complete practical joker, and I'd been victim to his pranks on many occasions. "Oh, I see you're back." I looked at him suspiciously, "Wow! Your observation skills really do amaze me sometimes!" I said, with a cheeky smile. "Not lost the cheek on your travels I see Jo? I'm glad I have bumped in to you, because I have a job for you." By this point, I was sitting at my desk signing some paperwork, so I put my pen down and looked up at him "Lee, seriously? I've not been back at work a day and you're giving me even more work? There are eighteen of us you know, not just me!" I couldn't believe that I'd snapped at him like that; I wanted to grab the words and push them back in my mouth! "Oooh, did someone get out of the wrong side of the bed, this morning?" Lee jeered "You don't even know what I was going to ask you to do!" I apologised, and he continued "For that attitude, you can make the brews before I tell you now." I guessed that was the least I could do.

I came back into the office armed with two cups of tea, and sat down at the desk. Lee stood up, closed the office door, and sat opposite me. "Right, what I'm about to ask has never been given to someone of your rank. I want you to go away and look at how Loyesford runs, and then put a business case together about how you would change it." I began smiling, because this intrigued me. Although the staff morale and teamwork was fantastic, Loyesford was an old jail, and in some ways seemed stuck in the dark ages. Loyesford had been built in 1801, whereas Ribbleton had been built in 1992. There were lots of suggestions that I could make already! "Not snapping now, are you?!" Lee continued, "I could always give it to one of the other seventeen managers if you'd prefer?" I asked why he'd chosen me. "The Deputy, Number One Governor and I all really like the way you think and work." I couldn't quite believe what I was hearing and was really flattered. "So are you interested then Jo?" I didn't even need to think about it and told Lee that my mind was already ticking away. He said he'd email me the terms of reference later, and with that, he stood up and left the office.

I wandered back down to the main wings, found Simon in his office, and told him what I'd just been asked to do. I had no idea where I was even going to start with a project this big. Simon sat and listened before he exclaimed "Jo, I hate you!" I laughed, "Thanks Hon, I love you too!" "Seriously, you really are the blue eyed girl in this place; you get all the good jobs! This is *huge*, Jo, and you could really make a name for yourself in the job with a project like this. If you can pull it off, that is!" I hadn't thought about it like that; I hadn't really had chance to think about it too much at all yet.

The following day, I was in my office when Pete, the Number One, came in. He started laughing as he pointed to a poster on the door which said simply

"Only positive attitudes allowed in here." "Morning Jo, I take it you put that up?" "Morning Governor, yes I did." I smiled "Jo, it's Pete, please. I understand that Lee has spoken to you?" "Yes, and about that, exactly how radical can I be in my proposal?" Pete walked over to my desk, picked up my stapler and hole punch, and put them together in front of me. "This is Loyesford prison as a whole," he explained, "The stapler is D wing and healthcare, and the hole punch is the remainder of the jail." Pete then passed me the hole punch "If you were me, and this was *your* prison, in theory you could do anything that you want on paper with it, but you can't touch D wing or Healthcare." I couldn't believe what I was hearing, "Seriously?" "Yes Jo," he confirmed "Go nuts!" "No pressure then?" I smiled "But why me, with something this huge?" "I've seen much less competent Governor grades than you in my time and I think you'll go far in this job; I'm curious to see what you'll come up with." Wow! What a compliment that was.

Over the next few days I threw some ideas down on paper and quickly realised that I had three options

- I could leave things as they currently were, meaning nothing would improve and nothing would change;
- I could agree with the current proposals to make minor changes within the prison; or
- I could be totally radical and change almost every area of the main jail, including tackling a huge taboo which would cause a stir with the staff: vulnerable prisoner reintegration into the normal occupancy wing. I knew this

would be controversial, but I was sure there would be benefits.

I ran my thoughts past Simon, and asked for his honest opinion. He thought that I was brave but 'mental' to want to integrate, and that I'd never get the staff or the prisoners to support such a plan. He did like some of my other ideas, such as a plan for early days in custody, and a two-stage induction process, but he thought I'd upset some people with my idea of using the resettlement area for workshops instead of the proposed pod system. I told Simon that as I doubted the ideas would all be accepted anyway, I may as well have some fun with them. I knew that the induction process I was proposing would be much better, because I had worked with that system at Ribbleton, but I decided that maybe I needed to start by phoning the Prison Monitoring Unit to find out if any of the local jails had already integrated their vulnerable prisoners.

I discovered that HMP Arley had an integrated system which had been running successfully for a few years, and also that HMP Heathfield were planning to introduce a similar model. So, the idea wasn't as crazy as I'd originally thought! I knew I needed to gather some stats on various things such as assault rates, as I knew these would influence any decision to go ahead when I handed my report over to Pete, Ray (the Deputy Governor) and Lee. I also wanted to see how the system ran in practice, so I contacted Arley and arranged to go and have a look. Then I decided to contact Heathfield as well, to talk with them about their plans for integration. At this point, I remembered that the current Deputy

Governor at Heathfield was Ian. It had been about two years since I had last spoken to Ian. I felt cheeky asking for his help again, but sent an email to confirm that they were indeed planning to integrate. It turned out the idea had been scrapped due to the cost, so I was left with Arley as my source of information.

August 18th, 2011

I'd had a relatively quiet birthday evening, knowing that the next day I would be visiting Arley with Lee. It was a very informative visit, and I took away lots of ideas. We left the jail at about 3pm, and Lee headed home, but I decided to nip into the Westfield Shopping Centre at Shepherds Bush. I wanted to treat myself to some new shoes because I'd been working so hard recently, and of course my birthday the day before gave me another excuse, not that I usually needed an excuse to buy shoes! The shopping centre was total shoe heaven! Here were all of my favourite designer shops under one roof: Gucci, Prada, Dior, Jimmy Choo and Christian LouBoutin! What more could a girl who adored shoes ask for? After about two hours of hunting, I fell in love with the most amazing pair of Jimmy Choos. It took all of my will power not to buy them, but even I couldn't justify the price tag, particularly as I thought back to my mum's earlier struggles to afford basic living essentials. I couldn't spend so much on an unnecessary luxury and left empty handed to get the train home.

The train home was packed, and I really did feel like a sardine squashed in a tin! I'd been standing at the front of the carriage, unable to move, for about fifteen minutes, when thankfully, after a few stops, the train began to empty. I looked down the carriage for a seat and suddenly spotted a familiar face sitting a few rows in front of me. It was Ian, so I waved and caught his eye and he invited me to sit next to him. I thought it was bizarre that I hadn't seen or spoken to him for about two years and then within the space of a few weeks I'd emailed him out of the blue and had now bumped into him again.

For the next half an hour or so we caught up on what we were each doing work wise. Ian asked about my project, and what my plans were. As I explained what I was working on, I decided to ask another favour of him, and Ian agreed that he would proofread my proposal for me. I was really grateful because the last thing I wanted was to look ridiculous when I presented it to my Governor. Then Ian looked at me and asked "So how are you, Jo? The last time I saw you, you weren't in a good place." I smiled and thought about my answer carefully, deciding that I wasn't yet ready to share my story with anyone I didn't really know "I'm fine, thank you, much happier in life now than I was back then!" As we approached Ian's stop, I thanked him again for agreeing to be my proof-reader, and said I would forward the proposal over to him when I was back in work.

The following morning, at about 8.30am, I forwarded my proposal over to Ian, for him to be my project critic. Unfortunately, Ian hadn't got back to me when, at 10am, Pete popped his head round my door and asked how I was getting along. I explained that

260

I had sent the proposal to a friend to proof for me and that I would get it to him shortly. "If it's that far along," he asserted, "I'll see it on my desk at 2pm, won't I?" I could see that he wasn't happy that I was having someone look over it before he'd had the opportunity to look at it himself. I didn't know what to say, so I said the only thing I could "Sure Pete, see you then." So I was going to have to jump in head first now anyway. Oh God, what if I made a total fool of myself? I walked up to Pete's office nervously, and was met by both Pete and Ray. I passed each of them a copy of my proposal and sat in silence while they read it. I was praying so hard that they would like it; I'd never been given anything as big as this in my life. If they were impressed, I was going to try and get some funding towards further improving my education and qualifications. Earlier in the year there had been the opportunity for free study through work, and I had completed an NVQ Level 3 in Management in just over three months. I was hoping I could go on to achieve Level 4 or even Level 5, so there was a lot resting on this moment; improving my education was another goal I was determined to achieve from my Bucket List.

I sat for what felt like an eternity, watching them reading my work. Every now and then, one of them would glance up at me, but they didn't say a word. Finally, Pete spoke "Jo, did you really do this?" Oh dear. "Why, don't you like it?" I asked nervously. Pete looked from me to Ray before speaking again. "I'm very impressed by what you've produced, Jo; I wasn't expecting something of this eminence." I couldn't believe me ears. I knew I had put a lot of effort into the project, but I had never anticipated praise like this. Ray was next to speak, "Jo, I'd like you to present this to the whole of the Senior Management Team at the next monthly meeting." Well I may have been 500% more confident than I'd been a couple of years ago, but the idea of presenting to every senior manager, and having to answer their questions and have my work scrutinized by them was something I felt in no way prepared or ready for! "Do I have a choice? If so, I would rather someone else present it." "Jo," Ray replied, "This is an excellent piece of work and *you* should take the credit for it, not give the credit to someone else." I guess that was that decision made for me then!

A couple of days later, I found out that Pete was about to retire, and Ray would be taking over as the Number One Governor. Two weeks later, I nervously attended the monthly Senior Management Meeting. I had armed myself with one of my famous Lime & Ginger Cheesecakes in hope that this would sweeten any negative comments I might have coming my way! (I also wanted some feedback; because this was one of the dishes I was planning to do in my upcoming MasterChef audition.) Thankfully, I was able to answer everything that was thrown at me clearly and confidently, and the feedback I received from my presentation was excellent. It was agreed that my proposals would save money and time, and would streamline tasks for staff while improving prisoner care (they loved the cheesecake too!). The following day, I was called up to the Governor's office, to meet with Ray and Lee. Ray looked at me earnestly, "As you know, we are very impressed with what you've put together. I've run this passed the Area Manager this morning, and we would like to implement your proposals." I looked from Ray to Lee and back again, waiting for them to crack and burst out laughing. I was speechless (yes, I know, *unusually for me*!), and was convinced this had to be a wind up. I finally managed a nervous "Are you serious?" when Ray prompted me to reply.

"We're deadly serious," he replied "And what's more, we'd like you to project manage the implementation of these changes over a twelve month period, with Lee as the Senior Reporting Officer." At this point, I was tempted to look under the table to see if Jeremy Beale was about to jump out at me shouting "You've been framed!" "Oh shit, you're really serious aren't you?" I put my hand to my mouth and apologised for swearing; I really couldn't believe this was happening to me! I asked if I could raise one question, and mentioned the funding I was hoping to secure for the NVQ Level 5, because I thought It likely that I would be able to get the work-based evidence I needed for Level 5 from this project. I was told I'd have to speak to Sue, the Business Partner, to find out what funds were available in the budget, but that I would have to be enrolled on a PRINCE2 Project Management course because the project would need to be run strictly according to those principles. I left the office completely dumbstruck.

Unfortunately, Sue confirmed that there was no funding available, but I decided I couldn't miss this opportunity and decided to fund the NVQ course myself. That evening at home, I called the assessor who had worked with me on the Level 3, but she was only able to assess up to Level 4, so I did some research and found a company that could do the Level 5. We arranged that someone called Mick would visit the following week to ascertain that I would be able to provide the relevant evidence for the level I was hoping to achieve.

Mick arrived to assess me on the same morning I was to hold my first project meeting, which was a bonus, because he would be able to see exactly what was involved. After the meeting, we went back to my office to discuss my options. I asked Mick if he thought there would be sufficient evidence for the Level 5 "Jo, you could evidence Level 7 with what you're taking on." he enthused! I wondered what that was the educational equivalent to, and Mick explained that it equated to a Master's Degree. I was stunned, and not at all sure I could pull it off. I had left school with just two GCSEs, in Music and Maths. Surely I wasn't intelligent enough to do this. Plus, would I really be able to tackle the extra work while working full time and taking on this massive project? I was bewildered, but suddenly remembered the time that Joy had lost her temper with me all those years ago, for not accepting or valuing my own intellect. "OK then, let's do it!"

Culinary Magic

After Mick had left, I sat in my office trying to take stock of what I was taking on board and wondering whether I could really achieve the monstrous goal I'd just set myself. I certainly don't do things by half, do I?

As the weeks went on, it became clear that I had actually overloaded myself; full time work, a massive project, my studies, MasterChef . . . and I'd also been successful in passing the first stage of an accelerated promotion scheme at work, with the full support of Ray and Lee.

I decided that the real danger was that I would end up, if I didn't simply crash and burn, as a jack of all trades, and master of none. I knew I wouldn't be able to do everything justice and give each role the time and effort it required. They were all amazing opportunities, and I was very keen to pursue each one, but I couldn't possibly do them all at the same time. I decided I would have to prioritize and put something on the back burner. I realised that the most important things to me at the time were the project and my education, and so reluctantly, I postponed both MasterChef and the promotion board, reasoning that I could always apply for them again at a later stage.

MYSELF, ME AND I

October 10th, 2011

I had tried, but sadly failed to get tickets to see Carmina Burana at the Albert Hall as a treat for Joy (for her birthday and Christmas), but we were still keen to get together because it had been so long since we'd last met up. We arranged a theatre trip instead.

Joy had arrived in Milton Keynes that afternoon, prior to our trip to London the following day; we were just catching up over some good wine before a potential lodger arrived to be interviewed. I'd had lodgers regularly since I had moved out of the house share and into my flat. I'd interviewed many lodgers over the years, and although I had always been happy to interview men, to date I had always chosen a female lodger, other than on occasions when it had been a man I'd already known through work or friends.

At 6pm, Nick walked through the door, and there was something about him that I instantly liked. My interviews usually only lasted ten minutes, because we all make decisions about other people very quickly, don't we? Nick was at the flat for over an hour, drinking wine with me and Joy. I couldn't stop laughing at his dry sense of humour and decided Nick was the right person to move in simply because of his cheek. I knew he would bring some fun into the house. At some stage, Joy had mentioned my cooking talents, and Nick cheekily asked if I would cook for him too. Previously, I had just charged for the room and bills, but I figured I could probably

266

work out a price to include food. "OK," I laughed, "But I draw the line at ironing your pants!"

Once Nick had left, Joy and I went out for dinner. As you know by now food had always been a passion of mine, albeit for a long time mainly in an unhealthy way. I was thankful for the culinary skills I'd developed over the years though. For example if I ask Becky where she wants to go to eat, she'll usually say, "Your house!" which was no problem as I still get immense pleasure from seeing people enjoying my food. I was really looking forward to going out to dinner for a change though, and the meal was fantastic. Considering the crap I had stuffed into my face time and time again, you might be surprised to hear that I was quite the food critic, and was more than happy to complain, in a not very English way, if I wasn't happy!

My starter that night was Devilled Mushrooms and Oh My God; I think I had a food orgasm right there and then in my mouth. As Joy and I debated the likely ingredients, I called the waiter over and with the backing of a few too many glasses of wine, and demanded that he get the chef for me. The chef came out of the kitchen a few minutes later. "Can I help you? Was everything alright?" I think he thought I was going to complain, but I smiled at him and told him that his starter was the most amazing thing I had ever tasted! His face lit up, and then I audaciously asked whether I could steal his recipe, because I was sooooo into food and thought I might "Simply die," if I couldn't eat those mushrooms again! The chef apologised, thanking me for my wonderful compliment, but telling me that he never gave his secrets away. Quick as a flash, in the middle of the busy restaurant, I got down on my knees and clasped my hands under my chin like I was praying, "Pleeeeaaaasssssssse!" I whined. He and Joy burst out laughing and he conceded that he couldn't say no to that, before asking Joy if I was always this mad. "There's never a dull moment with Jo in your life, that's for sure!" she answered. The chef headed back to the kitchen, only to reappear a few minutes later with the recipe written on a piece of paper. I thanked him effusely.

November 5th, 2011

Nick arrived on his moving-in day with a beautiful bunch of flowers and my favourite bottle of red wine. I was puzzled, and asked him why, but he said it was just a thank you for letting him move in with me. I was quite surprised, because I'd not expected something like that. Certainly none of my previous lodgers had arrived with gifts. When it was a female, I would usually put flowers and a welcome card in their room, but I didn't expect them to do anything for me. I was touched and speechless, thinking how lovely he was, but I also felt a bit mean: I had put a card in Nick's room, but no flowers or gift to welcome him. I helped him to bring his things in from the car, and showed him around – where everything was and how everything worked. I explained that we'd be having pizza for dinner that evening because I hadn't yet been shopping. "That's it!" he spluttered. "I'm moving out, and I want a full refund for you breaking our contract agreement already!" I wasn't sure if he was being serious and looked at him in shock, but he gave me a wink and

268

burst out laughing . . . Yes, we were really going to get along.

A few weeks later, I explained to Nick that I was going away with work for two weeks, "You can't," he cried. "How will I cope with out you? And more importantly who will cook for me? Seriously, I'll end up overdosing on Pot Noodles in your absence!" I laughed at him, because I now knew him well enough to have pre-empted his reaction. I grabbed his hand and walked him in to the kitchen, opening the freezer and pulling out the bottom drawer. I'd made him ten meals and written the cooking instructions on the top of the containers. "Jo, you're the best, you're like the Carlsberg of housemates; I'm never going to be able to find another housemate like you when my contract ends in MK." He hugged me and kissed the top of my head. This made me tense up briefly because I didn't know him well enough to feel comfortable with that level of intimacy. Nick sensed this, and quickly apologised, but I told him it was about me, not him and that we should talk. I felt I should explain about my issues so that he didn't feel awkward around me. He was a friendly and tactile person, but I wasn't used to men hugging and kissing me.

We sat in the lounge, and I told him some of my story; about past relationships; trust issues with men; and my eating problems. His face was a picture, and he was so apologetic, although I had to explain again that it was my problem, not his, and that I didn't want him to feel awkward around me. "Well," he reflected. "Now my new job in life is to prove to you that we're not all a bunch of bastards and there are still some good ones left." I laughed, "I'm a bastard-magnet believe me, and I agree with those who say that all the good men are either dead, married or gay. Besides, I'm committed to being a non-practising lesbian until March 2012." Nick laughed at me, "I'm neither dead, married, nor gay, and if you're a lesbian, that's fine, because I am a lesbian too, so if you need any tips or advice you can give Uncle Nick a call!" We really were like peas in a pod with our wit and humour. The following Sunday I drove up to Birmingham, where I would be working for the next couple of weeks delivering JSAC to potential Governors.

At the Birmingham assessment centre on the Monday morning, I was very aware that most of the people there knew each other already, but that I didn't know any of them. Thankfully, they were all very friendly towards me, but there was this one guy I couldn't keep my eyes off. I didn't fancy him, it wasn't that, but I couldn't explain why I kept looking in his direction; I felt like a weirdo or something! He clocked my glances and came over to sit beside me. Introducing himself as Barry, he asked if everything was OK because he'd noticed that I kept looking at him. Shit! Had it been that obvious?! Think quick Jo, think quick! "Oh, I'm really sorry. I thought we might have met before, because your face looks so familiar." He said he was sure we hadn't met (but I knew that!), because he'd never forget a face as pretty as mine. I smiled and apologised.

Over the next few days, I was still fighting a compelling urge to stare at Barry, and I still had no idea why! He was in his mid-sixties, a little chubby, and fairly plain. He wasn't unattractive, he was just . . .ordinary . . . so why was he so fascinating?! Barry approached me again one day, tapped me on the shoulder, and asked me to follow him. He took me into an unoccupied room and closed the door. I didn't know what to think or what to expect, but I didn't feel threatened. Barry asked me to sit next to him at a desk and then he picked up a piece of white A4 paper and drew red triangle on it. I was very puzzled when he handed the drawing to me. "I'm trying something, because I know why you keep staring at me," he explained. "I want you to clear your mind of everything, and then I want you to hold that piece of paper in front of you and really concentrate on it. I don't want you to think about anything else but that red triangle. When the time is right, I'll ask you a question and I want you to give me an answer."

I was listening, but my mind was racing, what was it all about? It was all very strange! I picked up the piece of paper just to conciliate him, but I was hoping we could hurry up and do whatever this was quickly because I was starting to feel a bit freaked out! As I sat staring at the red triangle, I tried to keep my mind clear, but I kept wondering what Barry's question would be. When he finally asked, "What colour is the triangle?" My reply was, "Oh fuck!" Barry asked me again, "Jo, what colour is the triangle?" I sat staring at the paper, "It's green, no wait, it's blue, no, it's a mixture of the two, like a vapour trail." "And what is the triangle doing?" Barry asked. "Ooooh, erm, it's moving, it's rotating clockwise." Barry burst out laughing and exclaimed

MYSELF, ME AND I

"I knew it!" I couldn't take my eyes off the paper, even though I couldn't believe what I was seeing.

Barry finally took the paper out of my hands, saying, "You're a sensitive kiddo." I asked him what he meant, but he answered my question with more of his own. "Do things like this happen often to you? Do you ever feel like you have been somewhere before but you know you haven't – have vivid experiences of déjà vu? Do you dream things that then happen, smell and sense or even see things you can't explain?" He seemed very serious. I told him this used to happen all the time, but asked what he meant about me being sensitive. Sensitive to what? "It's known as many things. People are called Psychics, Mediums, Healers . . . it doesn't matter what term is used, these people have gifts and so do you!" I sat looking at him without saying a word, trying to absorb what he had just told me. He continued, "Something will have happened in your life at some point to unlock your senses and spark your ability, probably something unpleasant like a near death experience, or you've had a very hard life that you've escaped from with drink or drugs. I don't need to know what it is, but think back to the first time something strange happened that you couldn't explain." I was already back in my bedroom on the night when the door flew open, not long after Annie first came in to my life. "Don't worry, everyone is born with this ability but most people just don't tune into it, and go about their everyday lives never knowing and not believing. I bet you sleepwalk too." "How did you know that?" I asked. Barry just sat there smiling at me.

That night, I got back to the hotel in a surreal daze; I couldn't take in my day and I wasn't sure what to think, feel or believe anymore. I'm not sure I've been able to express accurately in words what happened with Barry, but somehow it made total sense to me. The following day, he asked if he could try another 'little test' on me, which I allowed. Barry then asked me what my religious beliefs were.

I laughed, and explained that although I had been christened, I didn't regard myself as Christian because my parents had taken that decision for me before I'd been old enough to decide for myself. I only visited church for weddings, christenings and funerals. I concluded that I wasn't really a religious person. "Nor am I," Barry continued, "But do you believe in God?" I told him he'd regret asking me that, because I had quite strong opinions in that area. I explained to him that I didn't believe in God, nor did I believe in Heaven or Hell, I did believe that some people have twisted some religions, for acts evil – look at the wars caused in the name of religion, and look at 9/11. If God existed, why would we have so many starving people and so much devastating illness in the world? I knew I did believe in *something* though, I just wasn't sure what that something was. I didn't believe that death was the end, or what would be the point of life? I believed that our bodies were a vessel for the life that we were living now, but that when that vessel died, the essence from that person would continue until they found another life. I told Barry I thought there was beauty inside my madness and that he had been right to have suggested that I might have had a very shit life, to the point that about three years ago I had wanted to commit suicide. Thankfully, that hadn't happened, as I'd passed out on Jack Daniels instead. The following day my life had been saved by a man, an act of kindness, and a simple hug. That had been the turning point; the crossroads in my life; the point at which I'd chosen a different path. I concluded that with all the theories I had about life, maybe I was the reincarnation of Sigmund Freud! I went on to say that I knew I'd never have the answers to all these things, or maybe 'Allottville and my imagination' were just a very interesting place to be! Barry laughed, "I couldn't agree more or have worded that better myself. You're a very interesting person, Jo, and I could sit and talk to you all day, but I guess we'd best get back to work."

I had many more deep conversations with Barry during the rest of the time in Birmingham. As I was leaving on the last day, he handed me the two CDs I mentioned in the introduction. The ones I didn't listen to.

I got back home later that day and was in the kitchen doing dinner when I heard Nick come in the door. "Honey I'm home!" He bellowed, so I headed out of the kitchen with a cold beer, saying, "Dinner in about twenty minutes!" As I handed it to him. "God I've missed you," he said "Look at that for service! You're better than any man could ever wish for. Seriously, how are you single? My lunch is made; my dinner is on the table; I get a cold beer when I walk through the door from a long day at the office; you're easy going and funny; you let me watch sport on TV; you can hold an intelligent conversation and you have great taste in music!

Seriously, could you be anymore perfect? Will you be my wife?" I laughed at him, reminding him that I was still in my lesbian phase, but from that moment we became 'Flat Wife' and 'Flat Husband'.

I'd done nothing special for dinner, I'd just thrown together a homemade Chilli, making enough to eat now and freeze maybe four portions for a later date. But Nick ate the lot! It was this Chilli, and a comment from Nick, that got me thinking about the idea of starting my own business. After the first mouthful, Nick had turned to me and said "Oh my God, Jo, this has to be the best chilli I've ever tasted in my life!" I just laughed and responded, "Thanks Hon, but seriously, it's just a Chilli." "No Jo, you really should bottle your food and sell it; I've never tasted food as good as what you make even in some top restaurants." Again, I just laughed but all the while I was thinking . . . if only I could start my own business; I knew I would love to work with food, but could I do it? What did I know about running my own business or even about food production and sales? I'd never had any formal kind of training; I was self taught and had only learnt to cook because of my eating disorder.

Barry's CDs, by the way, had been tucked away in a drawer, and tucked away in my mind. I was scared to think about them, and focussed on other things in my life.

Shortly after this, I was having Thanksgiving dinner with my American friend Lauren and I broached the idea of a catering business with her. She was an amazing cook herself, and I asked her if she would be interested in starting a business with me. She said she was very interested, but nothing then really happened for another six months.

April, 2012

Lauren and I met up again for a cheese and wine afternoon and I mentioned the business idea again. We decided to go for it. I wanted to start the ball rolling straight away, and was really upset when I discovered that our first two choices of names for the business (Amuse-Bouche and Bouffe Chic) were already in use, but then one night I had a dream about my plans for the future and in the dream, I had called my business Culinary Magic.

I didn't think this name would be free for a minute, as I thought my other ideas had been more unusual, and they'd already gone. When I found that Culinary Magic was free, I immediately bought the domain name and registered the name at Companies House, it was as if fate had stepped into my life yet again.

May, 2012

Culinary Magic was established on Star Wars day! Not sure what the significance of that is, but I did feel there was some magical force helping me on my way! Unfortunately, Lauren didn't feel that she could make the necessary commitment and felt that I was far keener than she was, and so she told me that she thought it best if I carried on alone.

Almost straight away I had orders coming through the door, mainly from my LinkedIn profile page, where I had a solid base of friends and contacts already. I was incredibly nervous delivering my first business lunch in case I didn't do a good enough job. When I arrived at the office, I asked the manager to sample the food and give me some feedback. He asked me for an invoice because he hadn't yet paid, and I explained that he was my first paying customer and that I would prefer his party to be my guinea pigs and pay only if they were happy; if they weren't then they'd just had a free lunch. Later that evening, he emailed me asking for the invoice and saying it was amazing food. He also placed another order for two weeks later. Since setting up the business, I've received some amazing references, including one crowning me the Number One Cheesecake Maker in Milton Keynes! Out of the blue, Ian emailed me for a catch up, wondering if I'd left the prison service because he'd noticed LinkedIn updates about my new business.

June, 28th 2012

Then astonishingly, I bumped into him on the train again a couple of months later, when I was on my way back from a business meeting in East Croydon. As you know from the introduction, this was when he gave me ideas and advice about my new business that I hadn't thought of. Ian also gave me the inspiration to write my story down in the form of a book, *this* book. Had he never asked me what the tattoo on my thumb was, and what it meant, then I would never have told him my story and let him know the major role he had unwittingly played in it.

He wouldn't have known how his hug had literally changed my life, I would never have seen his reaction to my story and ultimately, this story wouldn't have been written.

My life carried on, but now, as well as a new business, I had a new sense of purpose . . . the telling of my story. It's amazed me how everything has flooded out since I started putting pen to paper (OK, fingers to iPad). It hasn't all been easy to articulate, and I haven't always enjoyed remembering the detail and some of the tragedy, but I hope you'll agree that I had a story to tell. Anyway, I haven't quite finished yet . . .

I was very sad when Nick moved back to Basingstoke when his contract in Milton Keynes ended. A few months later, a new lodger called Erica moved in. We got on (get on) well, but still I miss Nick's sarcastic wit.

August 6th, 2012

By now, I was storming ahead with writing this book, and having reached the description of my meeting with Barry, I decided to listen to his CDs. I'd been worrying for no reason, and had nothing to be afraid of. I don't now see 'dead people'. Was it really Sixth Sense that stopped me from listening to them sooner? Maybe, to some degree . . . but maybe also, as with other changes and decisions I've made along the way, I just had to wait until the time was right.

The CDs were called A Journey into the Light and Chakra Clearing.

Erica and I were watching a movie when suddenly I could feel the CDs calling to me. I had pulled them out about a week before and had told Erica the story about them and how they came to be in my possession. I'd been writing this book, and had explained that I was scared to listen to them because I didn't know what was on them, or what would happen to me if I listened to them. I'd put them on the shelf behind the sofa and continued writing. Something inside me, now told me, the time was right; I looked over at Erica and said "I need to do and I need to do it now." Erica rolled her eyes, muttered that it was fine, and left the room, to give me some privacy.

I loaded the first CD into my DVD player and lay on the lounge floor, putting a face mask on so that it would be dark as Barry had suggested. With the first CD, I was put into what I would describe a trance state or a deep meditation. I was fully aware of what was happening around me and could hear Erica moving around the house etc, but I couldn't do anything; it was almost as if I was frozen to the spot. Within moments, I almost felt myself being lifted out of my body; I wasn't scared, because I felt totally at one with the energy around me and at one with my own body and soul. I experienced something I can only describe as the most intense love I've ever felt in my life. I was filled with a perfect inner peace and an unconditional love far stronger than anything I have ever felt, but this experience was only temporary . . .

. . . next, I was taken on a journey. I was stood on

a little white bridge, going over a stream in a beautiful meadow, and I could see all the people who had touched my life over the hedge in the next field, as though they were there with me. Some had no faces, but I still knew who they were. I was then taken back to the night when I wanted to end everything and tears flowed down my face as though I was really there again, and could feel those raw emotions and that intense pain all over again, but could do nothing to stop it. The pain and hurt I was feeling felt so real, but it was also like a release and a final letting go of it.

When I finished that CD, I felt I'd better listen to the second one too. Now this one totally freaked me out! I'd never heard it before, and yet I knew every word that was coming before it was said; I was saying the words in my mind silently along with the voice on the disc almost as if I had listened to that CD thousands of times, but I never had! This CD talked me through my aura being cleansed, and then told me that angels were being put on the four corners of my home to protect me from any more harm and negativity; it went on to say that someone would visit me that night.

Before you ask, I had *not* been drinking . . .

I'm not sure if I dreamt what happened to me that night, but as I lay in bed, I think I was asleep but at the same time I was also totally aware of my surroundings. I was lying on my left side, when it felt like someone sat down next to me. I felt the pressure of someone sitting on the mattress. I couldn't open my eyes, as I was scared of what I might see, but at the same time I felt it was a peaceful presence and that it wouldn't harm me, so I didn't need to be afraid of it. I knew deep down inside that I was safe, so I decided to stop analysing what was happening and just go with it. I then remember feeling someone cuddling up to me and tucking the duvet in behind my neck. It was a very comforting feeling, and the person who used to do this was Jennie when we were young. The next thing I was waking up the following morning, feeling very happy and contented. . .

Those CD's were amazing and spiritually beautiful. They really were a journey in to the light, and I just wish I had listened to them sooner.

So the story of my journey draws to a close. Thank you for allowing me to share it with you. My tattoo, by the way, reads Cursum Percifico which means "My journey is complete." in Latin. I had this written when I came out of therapy, on my right thumb, at the side of what used to be my two purge fingers. I did this because I know that Annie will always be a part of me. She is my dark side, but she is a thing that I am now in control of one day at time, and each day that I don't binge and purge is a success. Don't get me wrong, I will *always* be bulimic but should I ever get the urge to purge again, I can look at my thumb and say "No, Jo, your journey is complete."

I am Jo

Someone who once read some of this story said to me, that they were amazed how I had functioned so long without sharing aspects of it with anyone. Yes it's true; I've had a lot to contend with in my life. But I would never change a thing that has happened to me. Why? Because if I did, then I wouldn't be the person that I am today. They say, what doesn't kill you makes you stronger and that I now truly believe.

The one thing that kept me going for all those years, apart from my mum, my sister and my wonderful friends, was my passion for music, from playing my trumpet and singing all those years ago, through to listening (and I mean *really* listening) to songs that are so powerful that when you close your eyes, the words make the hair on the back of your neck stand up and give you goose bumps; music that can reduce you to tears and take you on a journey. In fact, there is a special song for each chapter of this book; I guess you could call it the Jo Allott Compilation Album of My Life. I'm going to create a playlist and give it to my closest friends, family, and those who have played a part in this journey.

I will share one of these songs with you the reader and that is the song I chose for this chapter. I chose a song by U2 and the song I chose is 'Bad', the reason I decided on this was; if I could fight the battle I know you face I would, if I could set you free of the pain and suffering you are going through I would. Because life is simply amazing this side of an eating disorder and I can not wait to for you to experience it yourself.

Today, I am simply amazed at how extraordinarily different my life is and how much it has changed in just four short years *and all from a hug!* I really can't believe the things that I have achieved in such a short amount of time.

1 – I am now very happy, healthy and I know have an amazing future ahead of me;

2 – I've done incredibly well at work; in a job I absolutely love. I once said that I took this job thinking people would be more disturbed than me and make me look normal. But that is not the case, I actually enjoy the challenges that I am faced with everyday, I like being a positive role model, I love seeing people turn their lives around and most importantly helping others gives me such a purpose in life.

3 – I managed to get the educational equivalent to a masters degree in just nine months (still no idea how I did that!);

4 – I have established my own successful business; and

5 – I have written this book, in less than three months!

I thought I'd share with you what some of people in my life said when I first started this project:

Simon and Jo

I just wanted to say that it was lovely chatting to you today. I've only known you a short time, but I have seen that you have achieved so much in your life already, even with huge hurdles and I think you will achieve so much more. The book will be amazing, so make sure you finish it and never doubt in yourself again.

You have me in tears! That's going in the book . . .

I never get emotional, or should I say I rarely express my emotions, but I felt I really had to say something.

Emma, slap your husband around the head and tell him to get a grip ;0) x

Jo and Vicky

This trip down memory lane was painful; I WAS A LITTLE COW :0(

The past is past. I told you writing it would give you some kind of closure, but you've got to expect emotions too along the way.

Seriously I would have killed me. I am surprised anyone still talks to me, how does a child know and do these things?

Kind of innately, I guess, please don't beat yourself up. Kids are kids. Remember our talk on fate, it all happened for a reason to make you the person you are now - a lovely, imaginative, bright, clever, ambitious woman with a wonderful future ahead (remember me . . . when you're a zillionaire xx) Hope I've not made you cry?

Love ya, and no you haven't - sniffle sniffle x

Jo and Farah A.K.A. The Crazy Frog

Loved our chat today! Really inspirational! X I'm so proud of you and what you have achieved!! But seriously are you Wonder Woman or something? Xx

Thank you! I spoke to you because I see a lot of me in you, when I was your age and the potential problems you could face with you know what, I don't want you to make bad the choices I did. You're a

285

wonderful person and deserve the best in life - ALWAYS BELIEVE THAT! Failing this, my door's ALWAYS open x

Aww, your text was so meaningful and lovely! Thank you so much Jo x Love you x

Sam

Good Morning Jo, I just wanted to say that your book, or the bits I have read, is fabulous. It takes you through a host of emotions, sadness, fun, laughter and optimism. I want to read more! You really have a knack for writing. I'm also very impressed by your honesty and extremely intrigued to discover who 'The Man' is . . . Most of all, thank you for sharing it with me. You definitely are now 'I', Ms Jo Allott, CEO of Culinary Magic! Xxxxx

Jo and Ian

I've decided the reason you bumped in to me this evening is so that I can repay my Hug Debt by giving you access to the world's best cheesecake anytime you want it!

This is my top secret *recipe; if you ever give it away I will hunt you down with a sawn-off shot gun :0)*

Jo's Raspberry or Blueberry / White Chocolate Cheesecake:

Come on did you think I would really print the recipe in here? No chance!

Thanks for the attached. I will most certainly give it a go and your secret is safe with me, I promise!!

I was so inspired by you tonight that I came home and cooked myself the best salad I have ever made!!!! It was great and much better than chips :0)

Keep me informed on how things are going, it will be nice to watch you climb to your first million, and I am serious about the Bollinger!!

Keep in touch and hope to see you again soon.

Ian

Ian, have you made that cheesecake yet? Don't give me your saving it for a special occasion again! Everyday you are alive is a special occasion, because you never know when it will be your last! So get your pinny on please and make your wife a cheesecake :0) x

Becky and Jo

I just wanted to say to you that I am really proud to call you my friend and of everything that you are doing.

When you first started reading your story to me, I found myself thinking could I do that? Put my fingers down my throat just to lose weight. But the more of your struggles I heard; well, you have completely changed my own thought process about my own weight issues. You know that I have tried every new diet that comes on the market, but lately I've stopped that and I've found myself saying. I maybe fat, but at least I'm happy.

The book is excellent and really inspiring; thank you for allowing me to be the first person in the world to read it xxxx

Becky, you are my one of my dearest friends and you know I love you. But, you are getting telling off, which you had better listen too. YOU ARE NOT FAT! Jennie once said to me, it's just more of us to love! She was right xxxx

Jo to my Readers

I would now like to send a figurative hug to everyone out there who is having a hard time. I am no psychologist, or therapist; nor am I a self help guru. I am someone who was dealt an immensely difficult life path that pushed me to the brink, yet I have lived to tell my story which I hope will inspire others to help themselves. I hope I've shown you that you can turn you life around. I am living proof of that, and now that I have sorted out all my issues, my life is simply amazing! So it doesn't matter what your problem is, because it can always be fixed. If I can do it, with all the battles that I've had to face in my life, then I know that you can do it too. I have faith in you, even if you don't have faith in yourself yet. You just need to believe in yourself.

But I won't lie to you, it may take you a long time and it will require your total dedication. You'll have to face your fears, and stop running away from them. You'll need to start make healthy decisions, maybe for the first time in your life. It will take the strongest of will powers for you to be able to succeed, and you may fall off the wagon, which means that you'll have to start all over again. But that's fine, because you've already done it once, so I know you can do it again. It's not failing, it's just a glitch! You will need to push your body to the max, and it will demand the total sacrifice of the many temptations that you will be faced with along the way. It will hurt you like hell at times, but I promise you when you reach your final goal – IT WILL ALL HAVE BEEN WORTH IT!!!!

Until then, live well, be happy, let the people who wrong you go, wear a smile on your face and believe in yourself - FOR ONLY YOU ARE THE MASTER OF YOUR OWN DESTINY!

Hugs

Jx

Resources

www.b-eat.co.uk
0845 634 1414

www.balancedmk.co.uk
07716-755804

www.caraline.com
01582-457474